Adapt to Adopt

The Adopted Son of an Adopted Son

Trevon Howard

ISBN: 978-1-964852-46-1

Table of Contents

Preface

The story of The HeWill Foundation is not just about an organization; it is about a life lived with purpose, love, and unyielding commitment. This book, Adapt to Adopt: The Adopted Son of an Adopted Son, is a tribute to my father, Henery Wilson, whose journey from an adopted child to a father who chose me out of love has shaped not only my life but the lives of countless others.

My father, Henery, was more than just a man; he was a guiding light, a beacon of hope for those who had lost their way. His work as a program director and counselor in drug rehabilitation was more than a career- it was a calling. He dedicated his life to helping others overcome their struggles, believing deeply in the power of love and self-transformation.

He used to say, *"You have to love yourself enough to want to change,"* a philosophy that not only guided his work but also his life.

In many ways, this book is the story of how Henery Wilson became my father and why he chose to step into that role. It is also a story of how his love and teachings inspired me to create The He Will Foundation in his honor. The foundation's mission is to continue his legacy by supporting those who are overcoming life's challenges, whether through recovery from addiction or through the act of adopting or caring for children in need.

Writing this book has been an emotional journey, one that has allowed me to reflect on the profound impact my father had on my life and the lives of others. His story is one of resilience, compassion, and transformation-a testament to the belief that family is not just about blood, but about love, commitment, and the bonds we choose to create.

The He Will Foundation embodies these principles, honoring my father's legacy by recognizing those who, like him, have made the choice to change their lives or the lives of others for the better. Through this foundation, we celebrate the courage, strength, and love that define us as human beings and remind us that, no matter our circumstances, we have the power to create positive change.

This book is not just a recounting of events, but a celebration of a life lived with purpose and the incredible ripple effects that life has had. It is my hope that in reading this book, you will find inspiration, hope, and a deeper understanding of the transformative power of love and dedication.

In honor of Henery Wilson, and with gratitude for the life he lived and the lessons he taught, I invite you to join me on this journey – a journey that continues through the work of The He Will Foundation.

Chapter 1
Beginnings

"Family isn't about whose blood you carry. It's about who you love and who loves you." I heard this line in a family comedy movie once and realized how true it is. Having a mother or a father and not being family doesn't always mean the parents are at fault. You learn this at a very early age because, no matter how confusing things appear, children are extremely observant. I know this because I learned it at a very early age.

My birth father had suffered from sickle cell disease, and so did all of his fifteen brothers and sisters. It's an abnormality in the oxygen-carrying protein hemoglobin found in red blood cells. I never met all my uncles, aunts, and cousins because sickle cell disease limits your choices when it comes to living.

A lot of them passed away at a very young age. I had traits of sickle cell disease as well because it's a genetic disease. Me, one of my aunts and four to five cousins were the only ones who managed to survive this fatal disease. So it's kind of sad to have never met any of them because I belong to a very big family.

My mother, on the other hand, was a target of abuse by my grandfather, that left her traumatized and she found comfort in drugs and alcohol.

Despite all this, I never hated any of my parents. I believe that in better circumstances, we would have been a pretty happy family, but you don't always get what you want in life.

I remember my earliest days spent with my grandmother. My mother was lost to the grip of drugs, and my father drowned his sorrows in alcohol. As a child, these vices often left me alone and unattended, trying to understand the world around me despite being vulnerable to unseen dangers. I still vividly recall the story of that fateful day when, at the age of one and a half years old, my tiny hands found their way to a stash of drugs left carelessly within my reach. My innocent curiosity led to a near-fatal mistake: I ingested a high amount of drugs.

Naturally, my small body became unresponsive, with an overwhelming amount of poison coursing through my veins. My grandmother recounted how panic erupted around me as I was rushed to the hospital with a fifty-fifty chance of survival. Doctors worked feverishly to save me as my life hung by a thread. Miraculously, I survived, narrowly escaping death. This incident was a wake-up call for the authorities. They could no longer ignore the chaos that surrounded me due to my parents' addiction to life-threatening drugs. Consequently, they decided I needed a safer environment for the years to come, so they placed me in the care of my grandmother.

She welcomed me without hesitation and became my anchor, providing the stability I so desperately needed at that age and nurturing me back to health. Looking back now, I'm grateful that this decision was made because I don't know what kind of life I would have lived if that fateful incident hadn't occurred. Would I even be alive?

My grandmother did not live alone. She shared her home with some of her other children – she had a total of twelve kids. There was a man who would often visit the house. He wasn't a family member or even a distant relative, but something about him felt like family. Not only did my grandmother, uncles, and aunts consider him part of the family, but so did I. It didn't take long before I finally learned his name – Henery Wilson.

Henery Wilson may have been an ordinary person in the world, just existing like the rest of us, but in our community, he was considered a beacon of hope. He was a man whose mere presence brought a sense of stability and promise. I learned that he worked as a program director and counselor at a drug rehabilitation center, dedicating the majority of his life to helping others overcome their demons.

Seeing how he helped my family made me realize the profound and far-reaching impact he had on me. Henery had also helped my biological father, Ellis Howard, battle his own demons of drug addiction. Although I never had the chance to know my biological father, I grew up hearing stories of how Henery had helped him. Henery had a way of seeing the good in people, of recognizing their potential even when they couldn't see it themselves.

How did this impact my life? Henery's entrance into my life was almost serendipitous. He saw a young boy, lost and without a father figure, and decided to step in. At first, I called him Henery. He would take me out on Saturdays, showing me the world outside the confines of my grandmother's house. These outings were simple but meant the world to me. We would go to parks, visit museums, or sometimes just take long drives. Henery would talk to me about life, the importance of making good choices and believing in myself.

As time passed, our outings became more frequent. Saturdays turned into weekends, and weekends evolved into longer stays. Henery saw the void left by my absent parents and filled it with unwavering dedication. He understood my need for a father figure, someone who could guide me and show me what it meant to be a man. He became that person for me, not out of obligation but out of genuine care and love.

One day, as we were driving back to my grandmother's house, Henery asked me if I wanted to call him Dad. The question took me by surprise, but it also filled me with immense joy. At nine years old, in the fourth grade, I finally had someone I could call Dad. It surprised me because what he was asking was as casual as asking about the weather. No, this meant he thought of me as his son and even considered asking me to call him Dad. This wouldn't be a simple title to him; it meant having a father-son relationship built on mutual trust, love, and respect.

The surprise lasted only a short while, and soon I was overjoyed. At nine years old, in the fourth grade, I finally had someone I could call Dad. And just like that, my weekends with Henery became the highlight of my childhood. We shared stories, adventures, and lessons that shaped the person I would become.

It was through my dad that I learned about his own story, which resonated deeply with me. He had been adopted at birth by Leonard and Blanche Wilson, and his name had changed from Henery Coleman to Henery Wilson. Our shared experiences of adoption created a unique bond between us that only grew stronger. He understood the struggles and triumphs of being chosen, of finding family in unexpected places. His lessons were simple yet profound, and his belief in me became my strength.

Through my dad, I learned the value of compassion, discipline, and unwavering support. He taught me to strive for excellence in everything I do to be the best version of myself. Even as a child, I knew that his expectations were high, but I also knew that he believed in me. His belief became my strength, guiding me through each challenge I encountered while growing up.

Henery Wilson was the epitome of a Southern gentleman, exuding charm and elegance that left a lasting impression on everyone he met. His wardrobe was never dull; each row of folded clothes and hung suits described him as gracefully sophisticated, showcasing his impeccable taste. Once, I counted the shoes in his wardrobe and discovered that he owned over 150 pairs, each carefully selected to reflect his style and personality. Every time he stepped out, he was impeccably dressed, often in a three-piece suit with a perfectly tied tie and polished shoes. His appearance was always meticulous, reflecting the pride he took in himself and his Southern roots.

Despite his polished exterior, Henery was a man of humble demeanor. He carried himself with a quiet confidence that commanded respect without demanding it. I never saw him out of character. People addressed him as Mr. Wilson, showing the esteem in which he was held unless they were close enough to call him Henery. He didn't demand respect; he earned it through his actions and character.

But that wasn't all. Henery's personality blended mild-mannered patience with firm resolve. He spoke few words, but each word carried attention and meaning. His instructions were always clear and powerful, leaving no room for ambiguity. Through everyday conversations infused with his wisdom, he had a knack for making even the simplest lessons feel profound.

One of Henery's most remarkable traits was his ability to balance strictness with deep compassion and understanding. He could be stern when necessary, setting high standards and expecting the best from those around him, especially me. Yet, his strictness was never harsh or unkind; it stemmed from a genuine desire to see others succeed and reach their full potential. He understood the importance of discipline and structure, but he also knew when to show empathy and provide support.

Henery imparted invaluable lessons that shaped my life. He taught me how to think critically, how to learn from every experience, and how to stay true to myself. He instilled in me the importance of having a purpose, of pursuing something in life that drives you to excel. His belief in the power of desire and ambition was infectious. He often said that having a goal or a passion was the first step toward greatness because it provided direction and motivation for one's actions.

I always found Henery's teachings to be simple yet profound. He emphasized the value of hard work, integrity, and perseverance. He believed that success wasn't just about talent or luck but about persistently striving toward one's goals. His lessons weren't theoretical; he embodied them in his own life, demonstrating how challenging it was but how once understood, it became the easiest thing to do. His dedication to helping others, his commitment to his work, and his strong principles all exemplified the values he instilled in me.

In Henery, I found not only a father figure but also a mentor and role model. He showed me what it meant to live with dignity and purpose. His influence extended far beyond our personal relationship; it was evident in the lives he touched and the people he helped. Henery Wilson was a man who lived his values, leaving an indelible mark on my life and the lives of many others. His simplicity was profound, his lessons enduring, and his legacy one of strength, compassion, and unwavering support.

Henery's impact extended beyond our family. His work at the drug rehabilitation center was more than a job; it was his calling, as he used to say. He wanted people to see that life offered more than succumbing to drugs, and he ensured they saw it. People who walked into his office often felt they had hit rock bottom, lost and hopeless. Yet, when they left, their backs were straight, shoulders squared, and heads held high. Their eyes sparkled with the promise of a brighter future they could create for themselves.

I know this because I benefited from his mission.

Henery had a way of looking at you that made you feel truly seen. It was as if he could peer into your soul and rediscover the parts of you that you had forgotten or thought lost forever. His kindness was matched only by his determination to help others overcome their challenges. He believed in the potential for change in everyone, no matter how dire their circumstances appeared.

This was the man who adopted me, who chose to be my dad. He filled a void in my life that no one else could. From the moment he took me under his wing, I felt a sense of security and belonging that I had never known before. He became the most important person in my life, teaching me not just through words but through his actions. With his attention and unwavering support, he taught me to be the best version of myself and to strive for excellence in everything I do. His lessons weren't just about achieving success; they were about being a good person, treating others with respect and kindness, and never giving up on oneself.

Even as a child, I knew his expectations were high. He never settled for mediocrity and pushed me to reach my full potential. Yet, I also knew he believed in me, perhaps more than anyone else ever had. His belief became my strength, guiding me through the challenges of growing up. Whenever I faced difficulties, I could hear his voice in my mind, encouraging me to persevere and reminding me of my worth. He pushed me to strive for excellence in everything I did, but he also taught me compassion and empathy for others, shaping me into the person I am today.

It was a powerful motivator. It gave me the confidence to pursue my dreams and the resilience to overcome obstacles. His teachings were deeply ingrained in me, shaping my character and guiding my actions. He showed me that success wasn't just about what you achieved but about how you achieved it, about the values you held and the effort you put in. I learned the importance of hard work, integrity, and perseverance.

His life was a shining example of these principles, and his influence continues to inspire me to this day. Henery's legacy is one of strength, compassion, and belief in God. He touched the lives of countless individuals, helping them find their way and giving them hope for a better future.

Looking back, I realize how fortunate I was to have Henery in my life. He was more than just a father; he was a mentor, a guide, and a best friend, all wrapped up in one person whom I was fortunate enough to call Dad. One of the most profound lessons Henery imparted was that family isn't just about blood relations but about the connections we make and the love we share. He taught me that the bonds we form through compassion, understanding, and shared experiences are what truly defines a family.

He treated everyone he encountered with respect and kindness, always ready to lend a helping hand or a listening ear because he saw potential in every individual, no matter how lost or broken they felt. He understood their struggles and offered them genuine support, helping them find their way back to a healthier, more hopeful path. His ability to connect with people, to make them feel valued and capable of change, was nothing short of remarkable.

Perhaps that's why he saw something in me that I often couldn't see in myself. Maybe that's why he took me under his wing – because of our mutual experience of adoption after losing our parents or because he saw hidden potential in me. He believed in my abilities and gave me the confidence to pursue my dreams and overcome obstacles. Whenever I faced difficulties, I could hear his voice in my mind, urging me to persevere and reminding me of my worth. He pushed me to strive for excellence in everything I did, but he also taught me to be compassionate and empathetic toward others, shaping me into the person I am today.

In sharing this story, I hope to honor my dad's memory and the profound impact he had on my life and the lives of many others. As a human being, he inspired me to do better. His legacy lives on in the lessons he taught me and in the countless lives he touched, letting the world know what kind of person Henery Wilson truly was.

Chapter 2

The Curiosity Begins

Just because I lived with my maternal grandmother didn't mean I didn't want a relationship with my birth parents. I always did. Curiosity about my family has always been a part of me, and as I grew up, it became a lingering question: Where are my parents? Why am I not living with them? Did they not want me?

Growing up, I had no contact with my biological father and only sporadic contact with my mother. But I understand her. The things she went through in her life, the abuse and trauma at the hands of someone who was supposed to love and care for her—it's okay if she only found her peace in drugs. I don't blame her at all. I had my grandmother with me. She loved me to bits and fulfilled every wish a child of my age ever wished for.

However, I only met my father once. That meeting happened when I was in the fourth grade. I came home one day to find a man I had never seen before sitting in my grandmother's living room. He looked familiar to me, like a vague memory of my childhood. I remember staring at him, trying to pinpoint who he was until my grandmother told me. The air was thick with a strange mix of tension and anticipation. He was there to visit, something that was very rare given his fleeting presence.

My father. It was the only time I remember seeing him. The memory is hazy now, but the impact of that encounter stayed with me.

I remember the way he looked at me, his eyes filled with something I couldn't quite place. I remember how he was tall, with a stern but kind face, dressed in a way that suggested he had made an effort for this meeting. The lines on his face hinted at a life filled with struggles and perhaps regrets.

Certain moments stand out with crystal clarity. I remember the way he hesitated before speaking, the way he fidgeted with his hands as if trying to find the right words. I remember my grandmother talking to him, but I don't know what they talked about. I was busy staring at his face, astounded that the person sitting before me was my actual father. My real, biological father. He spoke to me softly, asking about school and my interests. It felt surreal, like a scene from a movie where the protagonist meets a long-lost relative.

There was an awkwardness between us. I was hesitant because my father was a stranger to me. He was silent, perhaps not knowing what to talk to his son about. It was an unspoken acknowledgment of the time lost and the gulf that had grown between us. My grandmother watched us from where she sat, her eyes bouncing from me to him, unsure how to handle the situation. She had always been protective, and I could sense her unease about this unexpected visit. Despite the strangeness of the encounter, there was a warmth in his voice, a sincerity that made me want to know more about him.

We didn't talk for long, perhaps hardly an hour or so. The conversation was surface-level, but the emotions ran deep. When he got up to leave, I remember he reached out and ruffled my hair. This little gesture felt both familiar and foreign. I don't know if it was my imagination or if it really did happen, but my father promised to visit again. It must be real because I sensed it was a promise that might not be kept.

That brief encounter stayed with me, becoming a pivotal moment that sparked a burning curiosity about my father's side of the family. Did I have aunts and uncles from my father's side? Did I have cousins? Why had he been absent? What was his life like? Did I have other relatives out there who might help fill the gaps in my understanding of who I was?

As I grew older, the questions about him and his family became more pressing. They never left my mind, always ringing louder and louder. It was like an itch that I needed to scratch no matter what.

The desire to uncover these answers became a driving force in my life. It led me to explore my heritage, to seek out connections with people I had never met but who were intrinsically linked to my identity. That fleeting visit, though brief and seemingly insignificant at the time, set me on a path of discovery that I hoped would shape my understanding of family and belonging.

It wasn't just about finding my father. It was about finding my place within that history, making sense of the past, and reconciling it with my present. The questions about my father and his side of the family became a quest for identity, where I planned to piece together the fragmented stories and build a fuller picture of who I was.

Years later, as an adult, I found myself dealing with medical issues that led me to question if they were hereditary. Sickle cell disease, among other concerns, drove me to seek answers from a side of the family I had no contact with. I remember my mother always telling me about my aunt—my biological dad's sister—Latavia Howard. She was eight years old when I was born and held me as a baby. I never met her either, and with how the majority of my aunts, uncles, and cousins died because of sickle cell disease, I wanted to meet her.

My curiosity about my father's family never simmered down. It was there, lingering like an unanswered question in the back of my mind. I knew almost nothing about that side of my heritage. The one fleeting encounter with my father in the fourth grade left me with more questions than answers. That is until a serendipitous event changed everything.

I finally landed a job where I tried to work as efficiently as I could to create a better future for myself, working at a cell phone company. It was an ordinary day at the call center, filled with the usual bustle of customer interactions and phone orders. In the middle of going about my tasks, one particular order caught my attention. A customer named Latavia Howard had ordered a phone through one of my employees. The name struck a chord deep within me. What were the chances that this Latavia Howard would be similar to my aunt? It seemed too coincidental for this to be just any Latavia Howard.

The name lingered in my mind, compelling me to take a chance and know more about it. It was a long shot, but something inside me urged me to act. Hesitantly, I asked my employee to inquire if this Latavia had a brother named Ellis. My employee looked at me, baffled, but complied with my request. It was a long shot, but it felt like fate.

The next time he called Latavia about the order confirmation and dispatching, he asked her the question, and for a moment, time seemed to stand still. I still remember the anticipation I felt; the air was filled with untold answers. The wait felt interminable, my heart pounding with hope. When my employee returned with a nod, confirming that Latavia indeed had a brother named Ellis, my world shifted.

I was flooded with emotions—excitement, nervousness, and a deep sense of connection. My father's name was Ellis Howard, and hearing that name linked to Latavia was like uncovering a hidden part of myself. It felt surreal like a dream that I had never dared to fully believe could come true.

Without hesitation, I asked to speak with her. When she came on the line, I introduced myself, explaining that I was her brother Ellis's son. There was a pause, a moment of realization, and then the conversation flowed. We talked about our family and the years we had lost.

Our conversation varied and was filled with joy and sadness as we bridged the gap that had separated us for so long. Latavia was warm and welcoming, eager to know more about me and to share stories about our family. She was as excited to have a nephew as I was excited to have an aunt. Sickle cell disease didn't give you much of a choice when it comes to living.

From that day on, Latavia and I kept in touch. We met in person, strengthening our bond and filling in the blanks of our history and lives. She told me more about my father and the type of person he was. Since she was much younger than my father, she knew only enough about him. I even had the honor of being at her wedding a few years later.

This serendipitous encounter not only reconnected me with my father's family but also helped me understand more about my identity and heritage. It was a beautiful and unexpected turn of events that filled a void I had felt for years. The curiosity that had simmered for so long was finally being satisfied.

On the other hand, my mother, despite her struggles with addiction, always remained a presence in my life. She would visit my maternal grandmother's house every few weeks or months. The custody battle between her and my grandmother was a painful chapter, and because of that, my younger brother, who was four years junior, stayed with my mother. I used to wonder why my grandmother didn't adopt him as she adopted me. Later, I learned that the traumatic past of my mother and how she was abused surfaced in court, hurting my grandmother as well.

But my grandmother made sure I lived the life that every child my age did. She ensured I received a private education and did everything in her power to shield me from the darker aspects of our family history. My grandmother, though not perfect, was a formidable woman. She had twelve children of her own and had faced incredible challenges in her lifetime, too.

My grandfather had a stroke in 1976, two years before I was born. This stroke left him partially paralyzed and unable to work. He was right-handed, and the right side of his body was paralyzed, resulting in him being unable to do the simplest tasks. Karma might have caught up to him because a man who had once been a black foreman for Amtrak, a prestigious position at the time, was now helpless. Naturally, they had him retire.

Despite his incapacitation, he continued to support the family financially through his pension. My grandmother, in turn, secured a job at Amtrak as a coach cleaner, eventually rising to the position of foreman. He managed to live around thirty to thirty-five years before eventually passing away.

The trauma my mother endured at the hands of her father, my grandfather, became the elephant in the room that no one wanted to address. My grandmother, often absent due to work, left the children in the care of their father, and he had failed them in the worst ways. The abuse they suffered left deep scars. My mother, one of twelve siblings, had to navigate this tumultuous environment while raising her own children.

But life went on, and my grandmother did her best to provide for us. I was the favorite nephew of many of my aunts and uncles, each stepping in to fill the gaps left by absent parents. Reflecting on these experiences, I realize how fortunate I was to have people like Henery and my grandmother in my life. They provided the foundation upon which I built my character, instilling values of integrity, hard work, and perseverance. Their influence, along with the love and support of my extended family, shaped me into the person I am today.

The grass isn't greener on the other side, but that doesn't mean it's always being watered correctly. I learned this lesson growing up.

Chapter 3

Meeting Trevon's Birth Family

Family is something that you're always connected with. My grandmother did get custody of me, but thankfully, I was never told to cut ties with my mother; I was always connected to my mom's side of the family, no matter the circumstances.

My grandmother raised me until I was 11 years old. My mother had me for only the first year and a half of my life before her struggles with drugs made it impossible for her to care for me. Consequently, I was sent to live with my grandmother, who became my primary caregiver.

My mother's visits were sporadic. She would come by every few weeks or once a month to spend time with me. I tried to cherish those times as much as I could, knowing I was too young to go and live with her—also, my grandmother wouldn't allow it for obvious reasons. Though my mother remained a presence in my life, she wasn't exactly a consistent caregiver. She didn't live with me, no matter how much I wanted her to.

When you go to school and see your friends describing their relationship with their mothers, you tend to feel left out and wonder where your life went wrong. So, I tried to cherish the moments she and I had. However, this situation created a complicated dynamic between my mother and grandmother. It never became vocal, but actions speak loud. I remember the tension between my grandmother and mother was strung so tight; I feared the day it would snap and all hell would break loose.

Ever since my grandmother had taken on the responsibility of raising me and became my primary guardian after learning about my mother's struggle with drugs, my mother felt a sense of loss and failure. It was understandable knowing that your own child wasn't with you. It was a burden on her shoulders, and she had to carry it alone. She never told anyone about it, but it was apparent. It was clear in the way she would come to visit and talk. It was evident when my grandmother would be around me whenever she was around. The atmosphere was suffocating because of the elephant in the room, which no one wanted to address.

Despite this underlying tension, my birth family was always around me. Even though I didn't live with my mother, my life was filled with the presence of my cousins, aunts, uncles, and, most importantly, my grandmother. I was enveloped in their love and support. Family gatherings, Sunday dinners, and everyday interactions kept me firmly connected to my roots.

My grandmother's house was a hub of activity. Every day, someone would visit or stop by for no apparent reason. It was like a pit stop. No day went by in silence. I don't remember ever seeing her house when it was only her and me. My cousins were like siblings, and my aunts and uncles were like additional parents. It was extremely crazy how loud the house was.

While living with my grandmother, my cousins, aunts, uncles, and grandmother constantly surrounded me. Their presence was a stable, comforting part of my life. However, what did feel hurtful was my relationship with my brother, Ernest. In the beginning, it wasn't like how I thought a brotherly relationship would be. It was different, tense, awkward, and, most of all, complicated.

He and I never lived together. While I was at my grandmother's house, he lived with my mom. He would visit my grandmother's house now and then, sometimes for a weekend or a few days. And just like how I'd excitedly wait for Mom to visit, I used to look forward to his visits as well. I had a brother, after all. Those occasional visits were special to me, sometimes with Mom and sometimes solo. We'd often hang out in my room, talking about nothing and everything. Those little moments created a bond between us, and soon, despite not living together, we became very close. We were very tight, and our connection grew stronger over the years.

During his visits, we would play together, talk, and just enjoy each other's company. With every visit, I could practically feel the development of our relationship becoming sturdier. I felt a strong sense of responsibility toward him as his older brother. Even at a young age, I knew I had to look out for him; after all, he was my younger brother. There is this natural instinct in the elder sibling when it comes to their younger sibling. For Ernest, I had to be protective, especially when I saw the challenges he faced at such a young age.

I remember riding my bike to my mom's place, which was about 15 blocks away from my grandmother's house on 76th, and speeding up my journey to my mother's place behind an upholstery shop on 91st and Western, just to check on him. My mother wasn't always around, and Ernest, just five or six years old, would often be left alone. It tore me up inside to see him like that, my baby brother so alone and confused, looking around in hopes that Mom would be back soon. Knowing my little brother was out there, unsupervised and vulnerable, drove me to take action.

I didn't want him to be alone, especially when he had an elder brother who loved him and cared about him. So, at the tender age of nine or ten, I would ride my bike through the neighborhood, asking the older guys—the pimps and hustlers—if they had seen Ernest. They would point me in his direction, and I would find him wandering the streets in tattered clothes. I would ride over to him and spend time with him, making sure he was safe. It was hard to see him wandering the streets looking lost while I was provided for.

I couldn't bear to leave him alone, so I would stay with him until my mother returned. Seeing my mother during these times was bittersweet. On one hand, I was relieved she was back; on the other, I was angry and frustrated that Ernest had to endure such neglect. But our mother was struggling with her own demons—abuses and traumas from her past, compounded by drug addiction and the fact that I was taken away from her.

These were tough times for all of us, but especially for Ernest. I remember feeling helpless, knowing that I couldn't do much to change the situation. I wanted to bring my brother back with me to my grandmother's house, but it wasn't that simple. It was heartbreaking. There were times when people would pick on Ernest, and I, despite my small stature, would step in to defend him. I was driven by a fierce protective instinct fueled by anger and a sense of injustice. I wanted to shield him from the harsh realities of our world, but I was just a child myself, after all.

I had to go back to my grandmother's house while Ernest remained in such a precarious situation. My grandmother and my mom already had a strained relationship, and the idea of taking Ernest away was fraught with difficulties. My mom's struggles with addiction and the trauma from her past made it hard for her to care for us.

My grandmother had stepped in once before to raise me, but she couldn't go through the same battle with the courts to get Ernest. The thought of another court battle, with all its emotional turmoil, was too much. This left him in a vulnerable position, and I felt the weight of that every time I had to leave him behind. It pained me deeply to know that I was safe and cared for while he was out there, exposed to so much danger, and I couldn't do anything about it.

Some older brother I am.

Even though I was unable to be there for him, our bond remained strong. Not a single strain was put on it, and we both made sure it never happened. We understood at a very young age that whatever we went through was something we couldn't control because we were kids. But we made a promise that once we were old enough to steer our lives in our own direction, things would do better.

We were brothers, blood-related, and that connection was unbreakable and unchangeable. We both understood the hardships we faced and found strength in our relationship. Even though I was just a child, I clearly understood the difficulty of our family dynamics. The desire to have Ernest live with us at my grandmother's house was always there, but the realities of our situation made it impossible. This often made me feel powerless at different moments in my life, knowing that as much as I wanted to protect my brother, I could only do so much.

These early years were crucial, shaping me according to my surroundings and the situations that I was facing in life. The understanding of family, responsibility, and resilience taught me the importance of staying connected, no matter the distance or difficulties. No man's an island, I know I have someone to work and thrive for. The tough times made it clear that he and I relied on each other and would do anything for our blood.

It was never easy growing up and fending for yourself. Life was pulling us in different directions, and sometimes, it felt like I was constantly running between my own responsibilities and trying to look out for him. All this back and forth made me realize that Ernest looked up to me despite how cruel our lives had been to us. When we hung out and talked about the things we'd do and how we'd be the last of the generation living the life we had been, I'd see admiration in his eyes.

I used to think it was because I was older, and younger siblings tend to consider their older siblings as their role models. It has me thinking that I have to be good not just for myself but for my brother as well because I want him to have a good life. I want him to never worry about the bare necessities of life. Every time I visit him, the way he looks at me as if I've hung the stars in the sky confirms the impact I had on him. In return, it was my responsibility and my new mission not to let him see his older brother being defeated in life. I wanted to set a good example and be someone he could rely on.

Even now, as adults, we are incredibly close. Our relationship, built on a foundation of problems and solutions, remains indestructible. Even though we didn't grow up in the same house, we were always there for each other, always connected by an unbreakable bond. We celebrate each other's successes, offer a shoulder to lean on during tough times and cherish the moments we spend together.

At the end of the day, when I sit in the quiet room and really think about my life and how I've lived it, I find that these experiences taught me that family is not just about living together under one roof. It's about being there for each other, no matter the circumstances, being each other's shoulder to cry on while also being their support to reach the top.

Chapter 4

The Legacy of Trevon's Father

When I first met Henery, I never imagined that he would become such a central figure in my life. Back then, he was just Henery—a family friend who often came around to share a cup of coffee with my grandma and chat with my aunts and uncles. He was nice, sure, but I didn't see him as anything more than the man who hung around the adults while I played with my cousins. Yet, he had this quiet, strong presence, the kind of guy who always seemed to know what to say to anyone in need. It was only later that I learned just how deeply he was involved in helping our family and how he would eventually help shape my life.

Henery wasn't just a family friend; he was also a drug rehab counselor who had worked his way up to becoming a director and running centers throughout his career. He had helped family members with addiction as well. My grandmother must have developed a close bond with Henery during those times, appreciating the way he helped her children when they were in need.

He didn't just see people as addicts or criminals; he saw them as individuals who had lost their way and needed someone to believe in them. This perspective shaped how I viewed people and the world around me. Henery taught me that everyone has a story and that everyone deserves a second chance.

He was someone who made my family members feel a bit lighter when he was there. I remember him laughing and talking with my grandma, sipping coffee, and sharing a smoke—moments that brought a sense of normalcy to our sometimes chaotic home. My grandmother, especially, seemed to form a bond with him, and you could tell there was a deep respect between them.

Then, one day, out of the blue, my grandmother asked if I wanted to get some ice cream with Henery. As a kid, the idea of ice cream was enough to excite me, but the invitation felt a bit odd. I didn't think much of it at the time; I just wanted that ice cream. Henery and I went out, and I remember how easy it was to be around him. We talked about ordinary things—nothing deep, just the kind of stuff a kid might discuss with an adult who was genuinely listening. It was a nice day.

The following Saturday, he came around again, and we went out once more. This quickly became a routine, something I started to look forward to every week. Henery would pick me up, and we'd explore somewhere new—Griffith Park, the zoo, or parts of Los Angeles I'd never seen before. For a kid from South Central, it felt like discovering a whole new world. I was amazed by everything he showed me, and those Saturdays became the highlight of my week. It resembled a father-son bonding experience.

At first, I didn't really think of Henery as a father figure. As a child, I didn't question it much; I was just having fun. He was just this cool guy who took me out and showed me a good time. But as the weeks turned into months and those months into years, something shifted. Henery wasn't merely taking me out for fun anymore; he was taking care of me, teaching me about life in his own quiet way. Before I knew it, he began asking if I wanted to spend the night at his place for the weekend, and eventually, that became our routine too.

By the time I was in fourth grade, Henery was more than just Henery to me. He had been taking me under his wing for a couple of years by then, and one day, on our way home from one of our outings, he said something that caught me completely off guard.

"You know, you can call me Dad if you want to," he said casually. I remember the day clearly; it caught me by surprise. I was stunned—happy, but stunned. Without even thinking, I began calling him Dad right then and there, and from that moment on, Henery was no longer just a family friend. He became my dad. I don't even remember ever calling him Henery after that day. It's funny because I know I used to, but now it feels like that name belongs to someone else. To me, he has always been Dad since that moment, and I've never looked back. Henery stepped into that role without hesitation, becoming the father I didn't know I needed.

I later learned that Henery had been through a lot himself, which likely made him the empathetic and understanding man he was. He was an Army veteran, having served overseas in Germany after high school. He graduated from Jackson State University in Mississippi with a degree in psychology, and even in the Army, he worked as a counselor. I believe that experience shaped him in many ways, giving him the tools to help others, including me.

Henery's ability to overcome adversity was something I looked up to, especially as I got older and faced my own challenges. He never sugarcoated life; he knew it could be tough, but he also understood that toughness could be met with even greater resilience. For him, it wasn't about how many times a person got knocked down but about how many times you got back up. He lived by those words every day.

The lessons I learned from him weren't taught in a traditional sense. My dad would talk for hours and I would just sit and listen. his perspective on life was different from anyone I've ever heard.

One of the most profound lessons I learned from Henery was the importance of generosity—not just in material terms, but in giving your time, attention, and heart to others. He had this incredible ability to make people feel seen and valued. It wasn't uncommon for him to invite someone over for a meal or to take someone out for coffee just to listen to their story. He believed in the power of connection and showed me that sometimes, the greatest gift you can give someone is simply being there.

But Henery's life wasn't without struggles. He had been adopted at birth, which I didn't fully understand until I was older, and I don't think Henery ever did either. His biological mother, Lucy Coleman, had given him up, even though she kept the other children she had with her first husband and more with her second. Henery was the only one given away. I can only imagine how difficult it must have been for him to be the one child cast aside and handed over to someone else. Despite that, he never spoke of it as a burden.

Although he loved and respected his adoptive parents, Leonard and Blanche Wilson, I think that loss stayed with him his whole life. Henery always made sure I knew about his adoptive parents, especially Blanche, who he spoke of with great love and admiration. He told me she was the one who taught him how to be a good father, and I believe that's where he learned the kind of love he showed me. Even though I have never met Leonard and Blanche Wilson, I feel like I know them because of the way Henery talked about them. They were my grandparents in spirit, if not by blood.

As I got older, I noticed that Henery stayed connected with his birth family more frequently, especially after Blanche passed away. He started reaching out to Lucy Coleman, his birth mother, and I observed how much effort he put into maintaining those ties despite the hurt he must have felt. He sent money, made calls, and even visited her when he could. He wanted to honor both the woman who raised him and the one who gave him life, even though the latter had relinquished him.

Henery's connection to his birth family was complicated, but he ensured I had a relationship with them too. He introduced me to his siblings and cousins, making sure I knew who they were and that I had some kind of connection to them, even though I was his son by choice, not by blood. It was his way of helping me understand the importance of family, even when things weren't perfect. I didn't meet most of his family until I was older, but I always knew about them because Henery kept those connections alive. That connection was important to him, and so it became important to me.

Looking back, I realize that Henery's experiences—both the good and the bad—shaped the way he raised me. He understood what it meant to feel like you didn't belong, and he made sure I never felt that way. He took on the role of my father without hesitation, giving me the love and guidance I needed, even when I didn't know I needed it. Henery might have started as just a family friend, but he became my dad in every way that mattered.

He taught me that family isn't just about blood; it's about who shows up, who stays, and who loves you unconditionally. Henery was all of that for me and more. In many ways, I think Henery's own experiences with adoption and feeling like the one left behind made him even more determined to be the best father he could be to me. He gave me a life rich in love and experiences—a life far different from the one I might have had otherwise. And for that, I will always be grateful.

Looking back now, I realize that Henery didn't just step into the role of a father—he became the father I needed. It all started with one ice cream outing. He provided stability when my world felt uncertain, guidance when I was lost, and love when I needed it most. He wasn't perfect, and neither was our journey together, but he was my dad. And in the end, that's all that mattered.

Chapter 5

Family Struggle

How do you describe an addiction? It is similar to the chains of dependency, where you feel shackled and unable to escape from its relentless grip. It's also a bottomless pit, one you can't climb out of no matter how hard you try.

For me, addiction is a silent thief. It sneaks into your life, often without warning, and before you know it, it has taken everything. It steals your sense of self, your peace, and your ability to dream. Yes, it is a bottomless pit too. Addiction has been in my family for a long time. My mom had her own past that drove her to seek solace in drugs. She lived a tough life. My biological dad turned to alcohol—his own way of coping, though he never touched drugs. So, for me, the roots of addiction ran deep. My biological parents were prisoners of their own addictions.

This chapter of my life was a dark one, filled with pain and struggle, but it didn't last long after my grandmother took me in. Until then, I didn't know that families could be different, that love didn't have to come with conditions or cruelty. I began to reflect on the concept of family. What did it really mean? For most of my life, "family" was something I didn't truly understand. My biological dad passed away, and my mom lived in a world of her own.

I learned that family is not just about shared genes or a common last name. Family is about connection, about the bonds we choose to forge and nurture. It's about the people who stand by you in your darkest moments, who see you at your worst and still believe in your best. It's about love, not as an obligation, but as a choice—one that we make every day.

And that is who Henery Wilson was.

When I was old enough to go to school, I felt lonelier than ever. At my grandmother's house, I had the privilege of being surrounded by relatives, but when school started, I realized it all came down to having parents and siblings. I would stand in the school pick-up zone and watch kids my age being picked up by one or both of their parents or sometimes by older siblings.

Yes, I had my grandmother, but she couldn't answer the unasked questions from those around me. People didn't say it out loud, but their glances spoke volumes. Their eyes asked the questions their mouths didn't. 'Where are his parents?', 'Does he have siblings?', 'He's always by himself.'

Everyone has two parents. I had one, but she wasn't available to pick me up either. So when I say my life was what it was, I mean it. I had to deal with the cards life dealt me. Even when my dad came into my life, I didn't feel the change until he officially adopted me.

Before him, my aunties—Carolyn, Alva, Ava, Judy, Yvonne—and all the other women, as well as my uncles and their wives—David and Auntie Holly, Pete and Auntie Rhonda, William and Auntie Carol—in the family stepped in when they noticed my loneliness. They knew I was missing something, and it was obvious what it was—love and belonging. They would often visit, showering me with love and kisses that made me giggle. They took it upon themselves to ensure I had a family and a place to call home, with people I could call my own.

But no matter how much love they gave me, the void in my heart remained. Even though I'm grateful to each one of them, it wasn't enough because, at that time, I was a child, and I wanted what other kids my age had.

I always knew my mom loved me, but she was just incapable of showing it because the demons from her past had a strong grip on her. I knew I was loved whenever she visited and talked to me. On the other hand, I've never really met my biological dad. I remember meeting him once, and that was it. I can't even recall his face, although I do have pictures of him. My mom used to tell me about him and how much he loved us. So, if circumstances were different, my parents would have been able to have a successful family.

This is one of the reasons why I call addiction a silent thief. It took away my chance to have a real family. But I understand that now. I may not have understood it at the time because I was a kid, with questions and tantrums. But now, with the wisdom of age, I understand that addiction is tough. However, understanding it didn't make it any easier to bear. If anything, it made it harder.

Then, when my dad—Henery—came into my life and showed me the true meaning of love and family, it was refreshing. It was a new experience; one I had never known. It was welcoming and soothing. I wanted more. I was greedy—a thirsty traveler in the desert searching for an oasis. It started as a mirage for me, only to become real, and I loved it.

My dad wasn't like other dads. He was different—my idol. He never married or had a family of his own. He never wanted that type of relationship with anyone. I used to think that was just life, making people live in different ways. So when he took me in and we developed this father-son bond, all the power and love he had stored within himself were directed toward me.

He was more than enough. He was better than both of my biological parents combined. He was everything I needed as a child, and I was glad to have him in my life. He made sure I had everything a child my age deserved and wished for.

Because of this, I didn't have to hide anything or pretend to be someone else to be loved and accepted by him. He accepted me as I was, with all my flaws, and gave me a home and love because he knew I craved that. That was enough to understand his actions, which expressed his wish and hope to be my father. My dad always told me he wanted a son, but he didn't want a relationship. So, I guess it worked out because I wanted a parent. We complemented each other.

My dad didn't want a marital relationship. He had trust issues. It wasn't that he didn't trust people, but he doubted their intentions, which made him distance himself from relationships. He didn't trust love because, according to him, if you love someone, you'd never let them go. Contrary to the popular saying about letting someone go if you love them.

For him, love could be taken away, so when he chose me, he knew I was choosing him as well. We were a team, united against the world. I remember I found a letter I once wrote to him while packing up his condo many years ago before I even started calling him Dad. I had forgotten about it until I later found it. In the letter, I wrote, "Henery, I want you to be my special friend and be with me. I don't want you to be anyone else's special friend." He kept that letter with him until the very end.

I wrote that letter at 6 or 7 years old. At that time, he was there for me in my life, and I wanted him to stay. He made sure he did. I didn't know asking him to be my special friend was my way of asking him to be my father. So when he casually asked me to call him Dad, I know now my message has gotten across, and he was being my dad the whole time.

After that, my days were filled with thoughts of Dad. I had someone I could rely on, and I knew that no matter what happened, he would be there for me and always love me. Suddenly, the world seemed to fade away, and so did all my issues. Life didn't seem as hard as it used to be. My mom's addiction no longer occupied most of my thoughts. All I could think about was having a dad and finally experiencing the life other kids my age had.

At that time, not having my brother around was not as painful because I had a dad, and I was on cloud nine. He eased most of my pain and hurt. He made sure I knew I had someone who loved me unconditionally. He was the oasis in the desert I was traversing. I realized that the universe works in mysterious ways—someone you never knew could suddenly become the reason for your well-being.

I could have lamented about my life, my parents, their addiction, and not having siblings to grow up with. I could have painted a picture of all the pain and trauma I endured, but my dad made sure he was the balm for all my wounds. He ensured that my past trauma didn't dictate my life. He helped me understand what was going on and made me strong, so I wouldn't fall down the same path.

That's who Henery Wilson was. He helped people without expecting anything in return. The love he had for me was truly exceptional. What he did for others, simply by offering his words and care, was profoundly inspiring. He didn't have to do what he did. It wasn't his responsibility. He didn't have to help anyone through their struggles or offer his opinion on how things could improve.

But he did. He could have continued on his way, but he didn't. He took his time with people. Even when it was inconvenient—when people got on his nerves—even when he didn't feel like it, he still helped. That's what he did for me, and I was his primary focus. He made sure I had everything I needed. My dad was the type of person who could heal a lot of the trauma someone had experienced.

In my life, he was everything. He took on many roles: my therapist, supporter, mentor, best friend, and father. He ensured I was cared for emotionally, spiritually, physically, and financially. He did his best to ensure my well-being.

The lessons from my adoptive father, the man who showed me what real love and kindness looked like, took deep root within me. Now, I realize that life is not always straightforward. My biological parents were meant to be my protectors, my first experience of love and security. But life had a different plan. With each passing year, as I grew, I understood that family, like so many things in life, is not defined by blood alone.

Family is a paradox. It can be both the source of our deepest pain and our greatest joy. It can wound us, nurture us, tear us down, or lift us up. The very people who should protect and love us unconditionally can sometimes be the ones who hurt us the most. This duality is what makes family relationships so complex and, at times, so difficult to navigate. Although it was not perfect, I'm grateful that I experienced the better part of having a family.

Chapter 6

Lessons from Dad

I remember one particular day when I was in ninth grade, a typical teenager who loved sports and was itching to prove myself on the basketball court. My friends and I would often stay after school to shoot hoops, dreaming of one day making it onto the school team.

The problem was, I was supposed to come straight home after school—no detours, no excuses. My dad had made this rule crystal clear. But on this particular day, the lure of the basketball court was too strong. I couldn't resist the urge to stay just a little longer, to play just one more game with my buddies. And, of course, that one more game turned into several, and before I knew it, I had missed the bus home.

Panic settled in as I realized the consequences of my actions. I knew my dad would be waiting, expecting me to walk through the door at the usual time. I had no good excuse for being late, and my mind raced as I boarded the next bus, trying to concoct a story that would explain my tardiness. Finally, I settled on what I thought was a believable lie: I would tell him I lost my transfer slip and had to borrow money from a friend to catch the next bus. Yes, that sounded plausible.

When I got home, the weight of the lie pressed down on me as I walked through the door. My dad was sitting in his usual spot, a look of calm expectation on his face. He asked me why I was late, and I launched into my story, trying to sound as sincere as possible. I told him about losing the transfer slip, about having to ask a friend for money, and about catching the next bus home.

I was confident that the words leaving my mouth would get me out of trouble. But as I spoke, I could see in his eyes that he didn't believe a word of it. He read me like an open book, his expression unchanged, but his eyes betraying the fact that he knew I was lying. Yet, he never called me out on it directly. Instead, with a calmness that made my stomach drop, he said, "Well, let's go see if we can find that transfer slip."

I froze. I hadn't expected this response. In my young mind, I thought the lie would be enough to get me off the hook, that he would accept my story and move on. But now, he was suggesting we go back to the bus stop to search for a slip of paper that I knew didn't exist. My mind raced, trying to figure out how I could escape this situation, but there was no way out.

Reluctantly, I agreed, and we headed out the door. The bus stop was a busy corner, bustling with people and traffic. Cars zoomed by, pedestrians hurried along, and the wind whipped through the street, carrying all manner of debris. I knew there was no transfer slip to be found, but I also knew that my dad wasn't going to let me off easy. At this point, none of my excuses would work.

When we arrived at the bus stop, he stood back, arms crossed, and watched as I began my futile search. I bent down, pretending to look for the slip, all the while knowing that this was a pointless exercise. The pressure mounted with every passing second, my heart pounding in my chest as I realized the depth of my mistake. My dad said nothing, just watched as I scoured the pavement, his silence speaking volumes.

At that moment, I knew he knew. He knew I was lying, and he knew I knew he knew. It was a standoff of sorts, a silent acknowledgment of the truth that hung between us. But he didn't call me out on it directly. Instead, he let me dig my own grave, so to speak, allowing me to experience the full weight of my deception.

After what felt like an eternity, I finally stood up, empty-handed and defeated. I couldn't keep up the charade any longer. The lie had crumbled under the pressure, and I was left standing there, exposed and ashamed. My dad's gaze was steady, unwavering, as he looked at me. He didn't have to say anything—his eyes said it all.

That was the thing about my dad. He wouldn't force the truth out of you, nor would he directly accuse you of lying. Somehow, he always knew. He would look you straight in the eyes when he spoke, making it impossible to turn away. If you tried, he'd shift to keep eye contact, ensuring you faced the truth.

We drove back home in silence, the air thick with unspoken words. I knew I had disappointed him, but I also knew that he had given me a chance to learn, to grow, and to understand the value of truth. In that quiet, powerful moment, I realized that the truth always comes to light, no matter how hard you try to bury it.

And I learned that my dad, in his own way, was teaching me a lesson far more valuable than any punishment could impart. He was teaching me the importance of honesty, integrity, and owning up to my actions, no matter the consequences. My dad was the kind of person who made you confront the truth within yourself, which made you honest in a way you couldn't escape.

My dad was a spiritual man. He had always raised me according to the Bible. He would sit me down and talk to me about God. I think he just wanted to raise me the way I needed to be raised, regardless of his own life circumstances and preferences. He wanted to make sure that whatever path I chose in life, it was the right one, and that I thrived.

He had that ability in him—to be a teacher and a counselor. And because of that ability, he inspired others to become counselors too. Take me, for example. I'm a motivator today because my dad guided me through life and motivated me to help others. He instilled in me a desire to give back, to support those around me.

My dad was a man of deep conviction. He truly believed in the lessons he taught me. Every interaction, every word he spoke, seemed carefully chosen to impart wisdom. He lived what he taught, and there was a certain power in that. You knew that if he was telling you something, it wasn't just idle talk. He embodied those values, and that made his lessons all the more impactful.

Growing up under his guidance, I found myself admiring him more and more with each passing day. There was something about the way he carried himself, the way he invested his time and energy into teaching me, that made me love him deeply. I felt cared for. I felt like I mattered. It wasn't just about the lessons themselves—it was the way he delivered them, with sincerity and dedication, that made even the simplest moments feel profound.

Even if we were just heading out to grab a bite to eat or taking a drive, the time spent with him was always genuine.

There was no pretense, no agenda—just a dad and son enjoying each other's company. It didn't matter what we were doing; what mattered was that we were together. Those moments, though they may have seemed ordinary to others, were filled with an extraordinary sense of connection and warmth. In these everyday interactions, I truly felt his love and care.

He always took the extra time to guide me, to show me the right path, even when it would have been easier to let things slide. He cared enough to make a point, ensuring I understood the importance of not "playing myself," as he would say. It wasn't just about the lesson itself; it was about the time and effort he put into making sure I learned it. That was his way of showing love, and it made all the difference in the world.

But it wasn't always serious business with him. One of the things I loved most about my dad was his sense of humor. He was a man who could make you laugh, often when you least expected it. He had this knack for cracking a joke in the subtlest way, catching you off guard with his quick wit. Though serious by nature, beneath that exterior was a subtle jokester who could lighten the mood with just a few words.

We laughed a lot together, and I took great joy in making him laugh too. It felt like a little victory every time I could break his serious demeanor and see him crack up. He had a way of delivering his jokes with a straight face, followed by a look that let you know he was just messing with you. It was all in good fun, never meant to hurt anyone's feelings. He was just smart like that, using humor as another way to connect and teach without ever being harsh.

One of the funniest moments we shared was watching *Ace Ventura: Pet Detective.* Jim Carrey was at his peak, and there was this scene where Carrey's character did something ridiculously silly—talking out of his rear end, as only Jim Carrey could pull off. I was laughing, but what really got me was seeing my dad, usually so serious, laughing so hard that we had to pause the movie. Tears streamed down his face, and I was amazed—I'd never seen him laugh like that before. It was one of those rare moments where I saw another side of him, a side that loved to let go and enjoy something utterly ridiculous.

That moment taught me something important too. It showed me that no matter how serious life can get, there's always room for laughter, always a reason to find joy even in the silliest things. My dad knew how to strike that balance—he was a man of discipline and seriousness, but he never lost sight of the lighter side of life. And in those moments of shared laughter, I felt an even deeper connection to him.

As a kid, it was nothing short of amazing to know the kind of person my dad was. I have so many good memories that I could probably spend hours recalling them all. But what stands out the most, what really sticks with me, are the lessons he taught and the way those lessons shaped the person I am today. When I look back at the good times, it's not just about the laughter or the fun moments, though there were plenty of those. It's about the substance, the depth, and the wisdom he imparted, often without even trying.

When I say my dad was a teacher, I don't mean he taught in a school. No, he wasn't a man who stood at a blackboard or handed out assignments. Teaching was just in his nature. He couldn't help but teach.

It was as if every time he opened his mouth, something worth learning would come out. It didn't matter what we were talking about—whether it was something serious or just some random topic—he always managed to turn the conversation into a lesson.

My dad had an incredible ability to weave teaching into the most ordinary conversations. If we were talking about cars, for instance, I'd end up learning something new about how an engine works or why certain tires are better in the rain. He wasn't consciously trying to educate me; it was just that he knew more about it than I did, and when he spoke, that knowledge naturally came through. It was effortless for him, almost as if he couldn't help but share what he knew.

There was never a sense that he was talking down to me or trying to show off how much he knew. It was just who he was—a man who had accumulated a wealth of knowledge over the years and was more than happy to share it, no matter how small or seemingly insignificant the topic. And I loved that about him. It made every conversation with him feel like an opportunity to learn something new and see the world from a different perspective.

Looking back, I realize my dad was teaching me something even more important: how to be a teacher myself. Not in the formal sense, but in how I interact with others, how I share what I know, and how I approach conversations with the intent to learn and to teach. He showed me that being a teacher isn't about standing in front of a classroom; it's about how you live your life, how you share your knowledge, and how you inspire others to learn and grow.

Chapter 7

His Influence

My dad had an aura that was impossible to ignore. He was the type of person you'd immediately notice, and if he didn't show up, you'd wonder where he was. You'd find yourself looking around, hoping to catch a glimpse of him because you wanted to see him. He was the life of the party. I think I'd run out of words to describe the man he was. Whenever someone asked me what kind of person Henery Wilson was, I'd just smile proudly and say, "Henery Wilson. My dad. That man was just… wow!"

And that was the truth. Everything he did in his life was amazing. He was the epitome of grace and style. He knew exactly what to say and how to say it, no matter the situation. His personality would leave you staring, wondering how a man could be so incredible. He had goals of his own, and every time we talked, he shared them with me. The way he spoke about his dreams made me believe that constantly talking about them would eventually manifest them.

I remember one of his dreams was to get a condo. We lived in a small one, but it was enough for both of us—a one-bedroom apartment, which meant we slept in the same room. But I never thought badly of it. I didn't care that I didn't have a room of my own or that I had to share it with him. For someone like me, who just wanted a family, I had everything I ever needed: my dad, and peaceful sleep. What else could I have asked for?

But by 10th grade, my dad saved up and he bought that condo. I was so proud and overjoyed at having my own room with my own bathroom! May dad has finally accomplished one of his goals.

My dad was the type of person who would never leave you behind. If he found out you were missing out on life, he'd grab your hand and make sure you enjoyed every waking second. I had never stepped out of the hood, where I spent most of my life before my dad decided it was high time he took me around LA and gave me the kind of experience every other child my age had.

Growing up in the hood, the sounds of bullets and shootouts were a daily occurrence. It was so normal for us that we didn't even flinch at the sound. But when my dad took me around LA for the first time, I remember my jaw dropping open. It was nothing like what I was used to. It was completely different. My dad brought me into a whole new world, and I couldn't contain my excitement. I wandered around, questioning everything, while my dad strolled behind me with a look that said how much he loved me and how glad he was to have brought me here.

Watching the sunset and walking down Hollywood Boulevard with him was a whole new experience. I remember thinking I was in heaven, the world around me so surreal. My dad introduced me to Los Angeles, and every experience with him growing up was just like Disney.

The other day, I was telling my kids about one of the memories that really stands out from my childhood—when my dad lost his car. It was a tough time for him. He had a small accident and ended up losing the car, and for a while, we couldn't afford to replace it. Now, my dad was the kind of man who didn't let anything hold him back. He was a proud man, always working hard, always finding a way to make things happen, no matter what. During that period, when he didn't have a car, he did what he had to do—he took the bus to work.

I'll never forget those mornings. We'd both catch the same bus—me heading to school, and him going to work. I'd get off at my stop, and he'd continue on, riding all the way to Hollywood where he worked. There was something so humbling and powerful about seeing my dad, this man who was always so strong and in control, sitting on that bus with me. He didn't complain; he didn't grumble about how unfair life was. He just did what needed to be done.

I remember thinking, *"My dad is on the bus."* It was a simple thought, but it spoke volumes to me. He wasn't too proud to take the bus, wasn't too proud to do whatever it took to keep moving forward. That's who he was. It didn't matter what the situation was; he was going to make it work. Seeing him on that bus taught me that it didn't matter what obstacles were in your way—you just had to keep going. And he did. He kept going, kept working, and kept providing, even when things were tough.

Hard work and patience really do pay off. Eventually, he got himself a new car—a black Thunderbird. I remember that car like it was yesterday. It was an '88 Thunderbird, sleek, with deep, glossy black paint. It wasn't the fanciest car, but to me, it was the coolest thing on four wheels. I was in high school at the time, and I was so proud of that car. My dad had worked hard to get it, and every time I saw it, I felt proud to have a dad like him.

There was a time in high school when I was taking this girl, Brandy, to the prom, and her mom had arranged a limo for us. It was great—it felt like we were living the high life. But the limo service ended at midnight, which meant that after the prom and the initial after-party, we'd be stuck unless we found another way to get around.

I remember asking my dad, "Can I use the black Thunderbird?" He looked at me with an expression that was a mix of surprise and reluctance. That car was his pride and joy, and here I was, asking to take it out for a late-night drive. I begged him, telling him I wanted to go back to the after-party by driving the car. I didn't let it go. I wanted to show off. My dad was hesitant at first, but eventually, he gave in. I think he saw how much it meant to me, and even though I could tell he wasn't thrilled about the idea, he handed over the keys.

I'll never forget the feeling of getting behind the wheel of that car, knowing that he trusted me with something so important to him. Driving that Thunderbird felt like a rite of passage. And believe me when

I say everyone loved that car. The black Thunderbird was the talk of the night, and I couldn't have been prouder. My dad had great taste in cars. As time went on, he eventually upgraded to a Mercedes S550, but that Thunderbird will always have a special place in my heart.

But the Thunderbird wasn't his ultimate goal. My dad always dreamed of owning a Bentley. He used to tell me, "Son, we're going to get me a Bentley one day. I want a Bentley." And every time he said it, I'd promise him that I'd work hard to get it. I promised him that I'd make millions and buy him the Bentley he always dreamed of. It became a running joke between us, but deep down, I was serious about it. I wanted to give him that Bentley, to show him that all his hard work and sacrifices had paid off.

A few years later, one day, he called me up and told me to come over. There was something he wanted to show me. I didn't think much of it at the time, but when I got there, he led me downstairs to the garage. He was grinning from ear to ear, with a proud, almost mischievous look in his eyes. He was practically bouncing with excitement.

We walked into the garage, and there it was—a glacier-white Bentley coupe, a 2007 Bentley GT. I was speechless. I couldn't believe what I was seeing. He'd done it. He'd gotten himself the car of his dreams. I just stood there, staring at that Bentley, feeling an overwhelming sense of pride and gratitude. My dad had always been the kind of man who led by example, showing me through his actions what it meant to be resilient and to keep pushing forward no matter what. And that Bentley, sitting there in the garage, was the culmination of all those lessons.

When he pulled up in one of those cars, it was an event. Everyone knew when my dad was coming. He didn't just pull up; he *pulled up*. There was no mistaking who it was. People would turn their heads, nod in recognition, and say, "Oh, that's Mr. Wilson." When he rolled up, you knew it was him. He had a way of commanding attention, and his cars were an extension of that.

To this day, I still have my dad's Mercedes S550, and every time I get behind the wheel, it's like he's right there with me. The car still smells like him—his cologne lingers in the leather. When I finally decided to sell the Bentley, I couldn't help but look over the paperwork and reflect on how much of the driving had been done by me. He had it for over 10 years, and in all that time, he'd put less than 3,000 miles on it. In the last decade of his life, my dad went blind and couldn't drive those cars, but that didn't stop him from caring for them. He'd go down to the garage, start them up, and let the engines roar to life, just to keep them in shape.

Whatever my dad did in his life wasn't for everyone else to see. He wanted it because it was an accomplishment for him, and that's what I think is important. The things he did weren't flashy for everyone to notice. He did them because that was who he was. My dad was born and raised in Vicksburg, Mississippi. He didn't come from wealth. He grew up in a time when being an African-American man in the Deep South wasn't easy, but he didn't let that define him. He built a life that he could be proud of, and in the process, he taught me what it meant to find purpose in everything you do.

My dad's life was a series of lessons in perseverance, determination, and resilience. He showed me that no matter where you start, it's where you finish that counts. And even though he's no longer here with me, his legacy lives on in everything I do. Every time I sit behind the wheel of that S550, every time I think about that Bentley or the old Thunderbird, I'm reminded of the incredible man my dad was and the lessons he taught me. He found purpose in his life, and in doing so, he helped me find mine.

As I look back on those memories, I realize that the best way I can honor my dad's legacy is by living my life with the same sense of purpose that he did. It's not about the cars, the money, or the material things. It's about finding what drives you and pursuing it with everything you've got. That's what my dad did, and that's what I strive to do every day. Because at the end of the day, that's what life is all about—finding your purpose and living it to the fullest.

Chapter 8

The Power of Faith

I'm not saying all this just because he was my dad and I loved him. Everyone around me—family, friends, even strangers—spoke highly of Henery. Whenever I meet someone and they find out I'm his son, they tell me what a great man Henery Wilson was and how fortunate they were to have crossed paths with him.

He left an impression on everyone he met, not by trying to, but simply by being who he was. His integrity, sense of duty, and compassion were evident in how he treated people, even those he barely knew.

We had a gathering where we shared stories and memories about my dad. This chapter tells the stories of some of Henery's mentees and closest employees. One of my dad's mentees, Lisa, told a story that, to me, perfectly captured his spirit. She didn't know Henery well at first. She only knew him as this polished, successful man who always seemed to have everything together. When they first met, she didn't even realize he knew her pastor. It reminded me how small the world is and how every encounter has a purpose in our lives.

One day, Henery visited her church, and she happened to be there, recently laid off and struggling to make ends meet. When he saw her, he gave her a look—half amusement, half curiosity, according to her.

He called her "little girl," and she responded with "Little Man," even though he was anything but small in stature or presence. They shared a laugh, and that was it—a brief moment of humor. But Henery wasn't the type to overlook anything.

Later, he pulled the pastor aside and asked about her. The pastor, perhaps sharing more than he should, told him that her name was Lisa and that she needed a job.

Without hesitation, Henery went back to my aunt and told her, "I wasn't planning on hiring anyone, but you seem like the kind of person who needs some work." Right then and there, he offered her a job. That was in 1996, and to this day, my aunt still volunteers and works in various community programs. She always says Henery changed her life—not just by giving her a job, but by offering her an opportunity, a second chance.

That was the essence of my dad. He didn't see people for who they were at that moment—he saw what they could become. He had a gift for recognizing potential, even when people couldn't see it in themselves. He wasn't just someone going through the motions of life; he was intentional with every interaction and decision.

Henery was more than just a man with a polished image. He came from nothing—his childhood was dark and difficult, the kind of experience most people struggle to survive, let alone overcome. But Henery didn't just survive—he thrived. And he made sure to bring others up with him. He saw the good in people, even when they couldn't see it in themselves.

My spiritual elder sister, Lila Rodriguez, mentioned that Henery was the most amazing person she had ever met. He became her mentor. At the time, she didn't think much of herself—she had been through more than most people should ever have to endure. But Henery saw past her struggles. He saw her heart, her potential, and her capacity to help others. He gave her a sense of self-worth. Through his belief in her, she found the strength to open programs that have since helped countless people.

She worked with my dad for about five years. When he first hired her, she was still trying to figure out her life. She told me how it all began: Henery asked her one day what she was doing with her life. She explained that she was going to school and living in a sober house, trying to balance everything.

At the time, she didn't think much of it. But Henery had a plan. The next day, he asked her to come back. She did, every day that week. By the end of the week, Henery told her, "You need a job." She hadn't realized how badly she needed stability—something beyond just surviving.

She laughs about it now. Back then, she was focused on school and staying clean. But Henery knew. He always knew what people needed, sometimes even better than they knew themselves. He didn't just offer her a job—he offered her a path. He saw her potential, something no one else had recognized, not even her.

He taught her more than just how to do a job. He taught her how to listen, how to be present for others, and how to grow out of selfishness and into service. She was young—just 23 years old—still learning the ropes of life. But Henery didn't hold her youth against her. He let her be young, allowed her to make mistakes, and when she did, he gently guided her back on course.

Henery taught her what it meant to be a good employee, but more importantly, how to be a better person. She would tell me stories of how he'd sit her down, not to scold her, but to talk through her missteps. That was classic Henery Wilson.

He raised me the same way. He never scolded; he let you figure out right and wrong through your own actions. If you felt ashamed, he'd simply say, "You're young. You'll figure it out. Just keep going." He didn't expect perfection—only progress. And that's what she gave him, bit by bit, day by day.

She loved him for that. He even became her daughter's godfather, and their bond grew deep. Her daughter adored him, considering him part of the family.

That was the thing about Henery. He didn't just touch one life—he touched many. He had a way of turning ordinary moments into life-changing ones. It wasn't just about business for him.

When he invested in someone, it was like planting seeds that would continue to grow long after he was gone. He helped people see their worth, showing them they were capable of so much more than they ever imagined.

Many people have come forward and said they've grown because of him. Henery made everyone around him realize that life isn't just about what you can do for yourself, but what you can do for others. That's something I strive to continue—to pass on what he gave me.

Henery had a gift for helping people, and he knew who needed it the most. He had an incredible spirit of discernment. He didn't waste time on people who weren't ready or sincere in their efforts to change. He could see through the lies and fakeness, and he wasn't afraid to call it out.

Another mentee said my dad didn't just want to change one person's life; he wanted a ripple effect. He knew that every life he touched would go on to touch others. His impact didn't end with the people he helped directly—it expanded with every act of kindness, every lesson shared, and every bit of wisdom passed down.

He was the man who understood the power of influence—the kind that comes not from status or wealth, but from integrity and heart. He didn't just live a good life; he helped others live theirs better. And for that, he will always be remembered.

Henery taught so much that I can't even put it all into words. I try every day to live by his lessons—to be as compassionate, strong, and discerning as he was.

One day, out of the blue, my dad casually asked me what I wanted to do. His voice was calm, filled with the wisdom that only comes from a life well-lived. I hesitated. I didn't know how to answer. The question seemed simple, but it was layered with complexity, and I felt the weight of it in my chest.

I said, "I want to stay near you." I thought he'd be angry, surprised, or at least hurt by my sudden words. But he didn't react the way I expected. There was no anger, no disappointment. Instead, he looked at me with those eyes that had seen it all and said, "Son, come back around, and if you ever need me, I'll be here for you."

That was my dad. His love and support were unwavering, whether you asked for it or not. He didn't need to say it over and over—it was just understood. His actions spoke louder than words.

That moment defined our relationship. Mr. Wilson didn't need to cling to anyone to make them stay, but he made sure they knew he would always be there. That kind of love changes a person. It changed me.

Chapter 9

Embracing Legacy

How many people here can honestly say they did more for my dad than he did for them? Not many. When you help someone, it's best not to expect anything in return, because more often than not, they won't. And it's not always out of selfishness or unkindness. Sometimes, those you help just need a small push to get their car started for life's journey. And my dad? He was often the passerby who lent them the strength to do so.

I remember times when I'd argue with him, insisting that it was okay not to be available for everyone. I told him he didn't need to be a superhero. Deep down, my protests stemmed from a childish feeling—I didn't want to share him with the world. I didn't want others to experience the same happiness and moments with him that I cherished.

But my dad would smile and say, "Being a superhero means saving those who need you." His mission was simple: to be there for others, to make sure they didn't feel alone, and to offer them hope when they had none. After hearing that, I never complained again.

It wasn't until after his death that I truly realized just how many lives my dad had touched. I organized his homecoming celebration and publicly invited anyone who had the fortune of crossing paths with him. I knew most of these people. But still the sheer number of attendees astonished me. And one by one, they shared their stories—stories only someone like Henery Wilson could inspire.

One man, Gregory, spoke with such reverence for my dad. He told me about the day they met in February 2002. Before Gregory even finished his story, I could see the admiration in his eyes. He had heard about my dad long before they met. He'd prayed about it, talked about it, and for years, he yearned for the chance to meet the man everyone on Skid Row seemed to revere.

"I always wanted to meet Mr. Wilson," he said with conviction, as if it had been a spiritual calling. And, as fate would have it, that February, Gregory's wish came true.

Gregory explained that he was enrolled in a rehabilitation program on Vermont, a place known for helping individuals turn their lives around. My dad had built a reputation as someone who would give endlessly, never asking for anything in return.

I knew exactly what kind of program Gregory meant because Dad had worked with so many people like him—people not just in need of help, but of hope. Gregory spent six months in that program, and five months in, my dad arrived on campus. That's when their paths finally crossed. It's amazing how small the world can be.

Just one month before Gregory was set to graduate from the program, my dad hired him, offering him not just a job, but a purpose. Gregory didn't realize it at the time, but that opportunity would mark the beginning of his own calling—helping others, just like my dad had always done. He told me that my dad didn't just see potential in him; he saw the spark that needed igniting.

Through Gregory, I learned how one person's actions can inspire others. Gregory loved helping people. He especially loved working with babies and seemed to have a heart big enough for everyone. My dad's influence was unmistakable. The work they did together on Skid Row shaped Gregory's life in profound ways. Over ten years of working there, Gregory earned his Ph.D. He dedicated his life to a mission like my dad's—helping people find their footing and doing the work most would shy away from. And he loved every minute of it.

That was my dad's gift—he took people under his wing and guided them effortlessly. Gregory often referred to Henery as his "spiritual dad," saying that my dad didn't just teach him about work, but about life too.

Gregory went on to work in social services for two decades. He told me that every lesson Henery imparted stayed with him. My dad's influence could be seen in everything Gregory did, from the way he interacted with others to how he handled difficult situations—with grace and patience.

At that gathering, person after person shared their memories of my dad. Gregory told me he had three mentors in his life. The first he lost in 1992. The second came into his life in his twenties, helping him when he needed it most. Then, at the perfect moment, my dad entered his life—almost like divine intervention. Gregory often said he had been lost, standing at a crossroads, unsure of how to move forward. And that's when my dad stepped in.

My dad had this incredible ability to make people feel seen and heard, no matter where they were in life. For Gregory, that meant everything.

He talked about how, even at his age, he still lived by the purpose my dad instilled in him: dedicating his life to helping others. Gregory wasn't interested in glory or recognition; his only desire was to give back and follow the same path my dad had shown him.

That's how Gregory carried forward my dad's legacy—by helping those who needed it most, just as my dad had helped him. He didn't view it as charity work. It was more personal, a reflection of the connection he shared with my dad. They lived together, but not in the typical sense. At first, I didn't fully understand what he meant, but now I do. He wasn't saying they were roommates; he was describing a bond of spirit, as close as family. For thirty years, they lived as neighbors, both physically and in purpose.

There was one thing Gregory always mentioned that resonated deeply with me. No matter how tough things got, no matter how dire the situation seemed, my dad would say something simple but powerful, a phrase he lived by: "Real good, real good." It was my dad's way of reassuring everyone around him, a reminder that even in the darkest moments, there was always something good to be found. That phrase stuck with Gregory, just as it stuck with me, and probably with so many others.

My dad truly believed that things could get better—that with enough hard work, faith, and determination, even the toughest situations could be turned around. He didn't just talk about this; he lived it, passing on this philosophy to everyone he met.

Henery Wilson was not an ordinary man. He was unique—chosen by God, as some would say, to help people in need. And he did just that. He was the kind of man who would run to save you instead of himself when the sky was falling down.

Another person who attended the gathering was Michelle, someone my dad had also helped. She told me she met him in 1992, on a day she hadn't anticipated would change her life. She had walked into the Jan Clayson Center with her children, waiting for a call, standing off to the side, when my dad noticed her. He approached her with that calm, unassuming presence that was so characteristic of him.

Michelle told me how he asked if she was alright, his voice so soft it was barely above a whisper. She said she felt like a small, lost child searching for her mother in a crowded mall. I couldn't help but smile at her description of my dad's voice. It wasn't just the words; it was how he spoke. Gentle. Patient. Even when he had to be firm with me, he never raised his voice. Michelle said she instantly liked the way he spoke— soothing and reassuring, as if, no matter how bad things seemed, there was always hope.

At that moment, Michelle was worried about her children, and my dad told her he had a son too. He explained that to discipline a child, you had to be calm and firm—not loud or forceful, not matching a child's stubbornness with your own. It wasn't about shouting or being harsh; it was about calmness, understanding, and teaching from a place of love, not anger.

This struck Michelle deeply. That was the kind of man my dad was. He had a gift for reaching people, even in their most difficult moments, making them feel seen, understood, and safe.

Within just five minutes of talking to him, Michelle found herself opening up to him. She had come to the center seeking help, but she hadn't realized just how much she needed it until she met Mr. Wilson. By the end of their conversation, he had become her counselor. Over the next six months, he guided her through the chaos she was facing in her life. She had initially come to get her kids back, to avoid going to jail, but what she gained from my dad went far beyond her original goals.

After six months, Michelle asked my dad for a 30-day extension—something that was highly unusual at the time. Most people came to the center, completed their program, and moved on. But Michelle wasn't ready to leave. She wanted to stay because she was not just putting her life back together; she was learning, growing, and becoming the person she wanted to be—the mother her children needed. My dad recognized this in her.

He granted her the extension. It was such a simple gesture, but to Michelle, it meant the world. With that extra time, she finally managed to get her life in order. She moved into a trailer park, got her kids back almost immediately, and for the first time in a long while, things started to look beautiful to her. The pieces of her life that once seemed shattered were now falling into place, and she credited much of that to my dad.

People often say we only come together when tragedy strikes, and while there's some truth to that, my dad brought people together for the best reasons—hope, healing, and transformation. He was there not just in the hard times but in the moments when people began reclaiming their lives, finding joy again, and building something better for themselves and their families.

Michelle often said that meeting my dad was one of the best things that ever happened to her. He helped her get her children back and, more importantly, taught her how to be a better person, a better mother, and someone who could give back to others. She carried the lessons she learned from him long after she left the Jan Clayson Center.

This is why I always stand tall with pride when people tell me how my dad helped them in some way. His ability to connect, to teach, and to uplift was unmatched. And even though he's gone now, the impact he made on people's lives will never be forgotten. He didn't just see people for who they were in that moment—he saw their potential, their capacity to grow, to become something greater. He saw what they could be, even when they couldn't see it for themselves. And that's the legacy he left behind.

When he passed away, I thought I'd never see him again, that he would live on only in my memories. But I was wrong. I see pieces of him in every person he ever helped. I see reflections of my dad's legacy everywhere. And that's the beauty of it—his legacy lives on, in the kindness he showed, in the hope he spread, and in the unwavering belief that, no matter how tough things get, there's always something "real good" to be found.

Chapter 10
A Well-Lived Life

Who would have known that a baby boy, born to Clyde and Lucy Coleman and later adopted by Leonard and Blanche Wilson, would one day change my life forever? Some people are born lucky, while others find their luck along the way. Despite the challenges I faced as a child, I've come to realize that I was one of the lucky ones. The circumstances of my early life and the struggles I endured eventually led me to meet the man who altered the course of my future: Henery Wilson.

If my mother hadn't struggled with addiction, or if my father hadn't passed away so early in my life, I might never have ended up living with my grandmother. I might never have crossed paths with my dad. While it's natural for any child to long for a loving, supportive, functional family, I've come to understand that sometimes the family you find is even more powerful than the one you're born into. For me, that family was Henery. He chose to raise me, and that choice—his willingness to take me under his wing—spoke volumes about the kind of man he was.

My dad had a profound impact on my life, not just through our conversations or the advice he gave me, but through the way he lived his life—through what I observed as I watched him move through the world with dignity and grace. My dad was a man of class, and he exuded it in everything he did. I always watched him closely, whether he knew it or not, and in those quiet moments, I learned some of the most important lessons of my life.

One of the earliest memories I have of my dad is how he dressed for work. Every day, without fail, he'd put on a clean, crisp suit and tie. He never cut corners when it came to his appearance. It wasn't about vanity—it was about professionalism. He taught me that how you present yourself to the world matters. It's not just about looking good; it's about showing respect for yourself and for those around you. His attention to detail and the care he took in ensuring everything was just right left a lasting impression on me.

Watching my dad get ready each day was like observing a master craftsman. He didn't just throw on clothes and walk out the door. There was a ritual to it. His shoes were always polished, his shirts freshly pressed, his tie perfectly knotted. He carried himself with a quiet confidence that made people stop and take notice. I remember thinking, "That's how I want to be when I grow up." And I did grow up emulating him in so many ways, from how I dressed to how I approached life.

But his lessons went far beyond how to dress for work. He taught me what it meant to be a man of integrity. He showed me the importance of doing things the right way, even when no one else was watching. He wasn't flashy, and he didn't seek attention, but people respected him because he was consistent. His word meant something, and in a world where people often make empty promises, that was rare. If my dad said he was going to do something, you could count on it being done.

Henery's impact on me wasn't just about the big moments or the dramatic changes. It was in the small, everyday things. It was in the way he listened when I talked, in the way he never raised his voice, even when I made mistakes. It was in the way he showed up for people, time and time again, without ever expecting anything in return. He had a quiet strength about him that made you feel safe, even when everything else in your life was falling apart.

Growing up, I didn't have the kind of stability most kids dream of. I didn't have a traditional family. But Henery showed me that family isn't just about blood—it's about love and about choosing to show up for someone, day after day, even when it's hard. That's exactly what he did for me. I can't help but feel grateful for everything he taught me. He didn't just teach me how to dress for work or how to carry myself with class—he taught me how to be a good person. He taught me that, no matter how broken your past may be, there's always hope for a better future.

Every little thing reminds me of him—his voice, his calm demeanor, the way he could make even the most chaotic moments feel manageable. Dad was the kind of person who left a mark on everyone he met, but his influence on me is something I carry with me every day. He was a positive person, always seeing the best in people and situations, even when it wasn't obvious.

I can still picture him watching me, observing my behavior, and with the softest nudge, correcting me. He never scolded or reprimanded; it was always a gentle push in the right direction, delivered in a way that was peaceful and easy to receive. That's a rare gift. So often, people try to force resolutions on others or approach problems with resistance and tension, but not Henery. Not my dad. He had a way about him that made you want to listen, want to change, without feeling defensive.

I listened to him—not just with my ears but with my heart. When he spoke, his words came from a place of genuine care. He wasn't just teaching me how to behave or handle situations; he was teaching me how to be a better person. And the greatest lesson I learned from him was how to be a father. He created another father in me. It's as if he reproduced himself in me, shaping my values, my approach to life, and my understanding of what it means to truly care for someone. Now, when I look at my own children or offer advice to someone in need, I realize that I'm walking in his footsteps. I am him, and he is me.

That's the beauty of his legacy—he didn't just influence the people around him; he created more people like him. He created that same spirit in me—the desire to give back and to guide others with the same patience and kindness he showed me. The reason I strive to be the man I am today, the father that I am, is because of the way Henery gave to me. I watched him quietly change lives—mine included—and it's that same quiet strength I hope to pass on to my children and to anyone who looks to me for guidance.

I often think about how fortunate I was to be on the receiving end of his wisdom. Henery never sought recognition, never asked for praise. He just did what needed to be done, always with a sense of purpose and humility. He saw potential in people, even when they couldn't see it in themselves, and he had this incredible ability to bring that potential out in a way that felt natural, almost effortless.

He lived his life in alignment with his values. He didn't preach one thing and do another—he walked his talk. Every day, he showed up, not just for himself but for everyone around him. And he did it in a way that made you want to do the same. It wasn't about being perfect; it was about being consistent—about showing up even when it was hard. That's something I try to emulate in my own life. I want to be the kind of person my children can look up to, the kind of father who doesn't just talk about being a good person but shows them what that looks like through my actions.

In many ways, Henery's greatest gift to me wasn't the lessons he taught directly, but the example he set. I learned more from watching him than I ever could have from any advice he gave. He was the living embodiment of integrity, kindness, and strength. And now, as I find myself in the role of a father, a mentor, and a guide, I realize that everything I am is, in large part, because of him.

So, when I say that Henery lives on in me, I mean it in the deepest sense. He gave me the tools to become the person I am today, and in doing so, he continues to live through me. His legacy is about the ripple effect he created—the way his kindness and guidance continue to spread through the people he helped.

My dad wasn't your typical man. He had this quiet wisdom about him, something that drew people in, no matter who they were or where they came from. He had a spiritual intuition that people seemed to trust, sometimes more than they trusted their own knowledge. There were multi-millionaires—people who had more money than they could ever spend in a lifetime—but when it came time to make a big decision, they wouldn't make a move without calling my dad first.

It didn't matter if it was a decision about something my dad had no expertise in. Real estate, for instance—he wasn't a real estate mogul by any means. But these people, with their empires and fortunes, would pick up the phone and ask him, "What do you think I should do about this deal?" They weren't asking for financial advice; what they wanted was his spiritual discernment. And even if he didn't have the technical knowledge on a subject, he had something far more valuable—guidance rooted deeply in his intuition and faith.

My dad had this incredible ability to sense whether something was good or bad, whether it would bring success or failure. It was a gut feeling, but more than that—it was his connection to something higher. He would listen to the person asking, pause for a moment, and then share his thoughts in the most straightforward way. And somehow, that advice always hit the mark.

People came to my dad because they trusted that his insight came from a place of truth, even if they didn't fully understand it themselves. There was no ego in his advice, no agenda. He wasn't interested in personal gain or prestige. He just wanted to help people, to guide them in a way that would bring them peace and clarity. And they knew that.

It always amazed me how these wealthy, powerful people, who could easily afford the best financial advisors and consultants, still felt the need to call my dad for guidance. They trusted him. That's the kind of power my dad had. He always had a way of making things clear, even in the most complicated situations. And he wasn't afraid to tell people when something didn't feel right.

That's what I try to carry with me now—that sense of calm and clarity. When people come to me for advice, whether it's my kids, friends, or anyone in need, I think about how my dad would handle it. He wouldn't rush. He wouldn't get caught up in the chaos of the situation. He'd take a breath, center himself, and then offer his thoughts with kindness and wisdom.

I strive to be that kind of person now. I want to be the one people can turn to, not because I have all the answers, but because I can help them find their own. My dad's legacy wasn't in the money he made or the success he achieved. His legacy was in the people he helped, the lives he touched, and the wisdom he passed down. And every time someone comes to me for advice, I feel like a piece of him is still with me, guiding me just as he guided them. In that way, he continues to live on—not just in me, but in everyone he helped along the way.

My dad died a physical death on October 17, 2022. But I tell you from the bottom of my heart. His spirit lives in me and the lives he touched.

Henery Wilson shaped my life. He took a boy and showed him a different path. I can still hear his voice sometimes, soft and gentle, guiding me, reminding me of the lessons he taught me so many years ago. It was never about him—it was always about how he could help you. And every time I put on a suit, every time I take a moment to do things the right way, I know that a part of Henery is still with me. Henery did that for me, and now, it's my turn to do the same.

Chapter 11

"Henery's key lesson's for living a good life"

This book is written in honor of a man whose life was built on love, faith, and the power of choice—my father, Henry Wilson. His words, actions, and deep belief in the potential of people shaped everything I do, and it's that legacy I want to share with you.

Through his journey, my father encountered individuals facing life's hardest battles: addiction, loss, and adversity. But his guiding principle was always the same: "He will if you will." In other words, you have the power to create change in your life. God will help you, but only if you make the choice to help yourself. My father taught me that success and fulfillment come not from waiting for life to improve but from making the conscious decision to improve it.

In this book, you'll find the wisdom of his sayings, each one a call to recognize your inner strength, overcome your obstacles, and lift others up with you. These words aren't just motivational quotes; they are action-driven philosophies meant to challenge you, ignite your potential, and inspire you to act—first for yourself, and then for those around you.

This book is about transformation—yours and the lives you touch. It's about understanding that, as my father said, "Life is as good as YOU want it to be." And it's about realizing that the power to make life better is already in your hands.

"Let No Man Be Your God"

Taking Ownership of Your Life

The first and most critical lesson my father taught me was this: "Let no man be your God." It's a powerful call to take full responsibility for your life. No one else gets to define your worth, happiness, or success— not your boss, family, or friends. This life is yours, and only you have the authority to shape it.

Many of us hand over our power without realizing it. We let others' opinions guide our decisions, seek validation from external sources, and live our lives trying to meet someone else's expectations. But the truth is, the only person you need validation from is yourself. The moment you realize that no one has control over your happiness but you is the moment you become truly free.

You are the architect of your life. You decide the structure, the foundation, and the design. You decide whether you live with purpose or drift along, carried by the currents of someone else's agenda. "Let no man be your God" doesn't mean you shouldn't seek advice, love, or guidance from others—it means you should never allow another person's voice to override your own inner truth.

My father used this saying to teach me the importance of self-reliance and internal strength. He believed in people, but he also believed in personal accountability. He would often say, "God gave you the ability to be happy—who or what can make you unhappy if you don't let them?" This wasn't just about controlling emotions; it was about recognizing your power to shape your own life.

The world is full of people who will try to tell you what you can and cannot do, who will try to impose their limits on you. But the truth is, only you know your potential, and only you can decide what your life will be. The moment you take responsibility for your life is the moment you realize that no one else has the power to make you fail—or succeed.

Start today by reclaiming that power. Recognize that you are not here to fulfill someone else's expectations. You are here to live your truth, create a life that reflects your values, and decide what success means to you. The only validation you need comes from within.

"You Either Work in the Beginning and Play in the End, or Play in the Beginning and Work in the End"

The Power of Discipline and Focus

Life is a series of choices. My father believed that one of the most important choices you make is when to work and when to play. He often said, "You either work in the beginning and play in the end, or play in the beginning and work in the end." This simple phrase carries profound wisdom: discipline and hard work today lead to freedom and enjoyment tomorrow.

In today's world, we are constantly bombarded with distractions. Instant gratification is at our fingertips, and the temptation to "play now, work later" is ever-present. But this is where discipline comes in. When you choose to work hard and focus on your goals early in life, you set the stage for future success and freedom. On the other hand, if you spend your early years chasing pleasure without purpose, you may find yourself working twice as hard later, when the stakes are higher, and time is shorter.

The message is clear: invest in your future by making the sacrifices now. This isn't just about financial success—it's about building the life you want. Whether it's your career, relationships, or personal growth, the effort you put in today will determine the freedom you experience tomorrow.

Hard work and discipline aren't glamorous. They aren't always fun. But they are necessary. My father understood that, and he lived it. He worked tirelessly to build a life where he could provide for his family and have the freedom to enjoy the fruits of his labor. But he never compromised on one truth: if you want a life of joy and fulfillment, you have to be willing to put in the work now.

"Always Be Thankful for a Good and Loving God"

Gratitude and Faith in Every Step

In life, we often focus on the things we don't have—the opportunities that slipped away, the challenges that feel unfair, or the goals that seem impossible to reach. But my father had a saying that changed my perspective: "Always be thankful for a good and loving God." This was more than just a phrase; it was a philosophy that carried him through his toughest times and reminded him, and everyone around him, that gratitude is a transformative force.

Gratitude is not about ignoring the hard times or pretending that everything is perfect. It's about recognizing the good in your life, no matter how small, and trusting that there is a purpose behind every challenge you face. Gratitude opens your eyes to the blessings you already have, even when life feels heavy. It shifts your focus from what's missing to what's already present, and from that space, peace and strength are born.

The practice of gratitude is not just about feeling good—it's about creating a mindset that allows you to handle adversity with grace. When you're thankful for the good and loving God that guides your life, you begin to see that every hardship is an opportunity for growth, every setback is a chance to develop resilience, and every victory, no matter how small, is worth celebrating.

Gratitude Is Power

Many people misunderstand gratitude. They think it's about being happy only when things go well. But true gratitude—the kind my father embodied—is much deeper. It's easy to be thankful when life is smooth, when the job is secure, the relationships are strong, and your health is good. But the real power of gratitude is found when things aren't going your way.

When you're facing uncertainty, disappointment, or even pain, gratitude helps you keep perspective. It reminds you that, despite your current struggles, there is still good in your life. Gratitude helps you focus on what you do have control over, and it fuels resilience because you realize that your struggles are temporary, but the goodness of God is eternal.

Think about a time when you were going through something difficult. Maybe you lost someone close to you, or you faced a career setback. In those moments, it's easy to spiral into negativity, to feel like life is unfair, or that you've been dealt a bad hand. But what if, in that moment, you chose gratitude instead? What if you looked for even the smallest blessing—whether it's a supportive friend, your health, or simply the fact that you woke up this morning with the chance to start again?

Choosing gratitude doesn't mean dismissing your pain. It means acknowledging that there is still good, even in the hardest of times. Gratitude allows you to shift your perspective from one of lack to one of abundance. It keeps you grounded and reminds you that no matter how challenging your current situation, God's love and goodness remain.

Faith as Your Anchor

Gratitude is tied directly to faith. When you trust in a good and loving God, you can face any challenge with the knowledge that there is a higher purpose behind it. My father often reminded me that faith and gratitude were inseparable. You can't have true gratitude without faith—faith that everything happens for a reason, faith that you are where you are supposed to be, and faith that God's love is guiding you toward something greater, even if you can't see it yet.

Faith is your anchor. It holds you steady when life's storms come. It keeps you grounded in the belief that no matter how hard things get, God's plan is unfolding in ways you may not yet understand. Gratitude, then, becomes an expression of that faith. It's your way of saying, "I trust that this is part of my journey. I trust that even in this challenge, there is something for me to learn, something that will make me stronger."

When you live in gratitude, you're not just thankful for the obvious blessings. You're thankful for the journey itself—the highs, the lows, and everything in between. You begin to realize that even the hardest moments are shaping you into the person you're meant to be.

Building a Gratitude Practice

Gratitude, like any powerful habit, needs to be practiced. It's not enough to say "thank you" when things are going well. You need to build it into your daily life. My father believed that one of the keys to his peace of mind was his daily practice of gratitude. He would start and end each day with a moment of reflection, thanking God for the opportunities and lessons that the day had brought him. This practice gave him clarity, even in difficult times.

Here's how you can start building your own gratitude practice:

- **Daily Reflection**: Each morning or evening, take five minutes to reflect on three things you're grateful for. They don't have to be big or profound—sometimes the simplest things, like a warm cup of coffee or a good conversation, can shift your mindset.

- **Gratitude Journal**: Keep a journal where you write down what you're thankful for each day. This helps reinforce the habit and gives you a tangible reminder of the good in your life.

- **Express Your Gratitude**: Don't just keep gratitude to yourself—share it. Tell the people around you how much you appreciate them. Gratitude, when expressed outwardly, not only lifts your spirits but strengthens your relationships.

Living a life of gratitude doesn't just make you feel good—it changes the way you see the world. It opens your heart to the beauty in every moment and connects you more deeply to the people around you. Most importantly, it strengthens your faith in a good and loving God, and that faith will carry you through even the darkest of times.

"Life Is as Good as You Want It to Be"

Taking Control of Your Reality

We all have moments when we feel stuck, like life isn't turning out the way we had hoped. Maybe you're in a job that doesn't fulfill you, a relationship that isn't working, or you're struggling with personal challenges that feel overwhelming. But there's a truth my father often repeated, a truth that can change everything: "Life is as good as you want it to be."

This saying isn't about ignoring hardships or pretending life will magically become perfect. It's about recognizing that you have the power to shape your own experience. Your attitude, choices, and actions define your life. External circumstances may be out of your control, but how you respond to them is entirely up to you.

Your Mindset Shapes Your World

Your mindset is the lens through which you see the world. If you believe life is full of opportunities, you'll find them everywhere. But if you believe life is full of obstacles, that's all you'll see. My father taught me that the key to creating a good life starts with choosing a positive, empowered mindset.

Life will always present challenges—that's inevitable. But the people who succeed—the ones who live fulfilling, meaningful lives—are those who choose to see challenges as opportunities for growth. They don't let setbacks define them. Instead, they ask, "What can I learn from this? How can I use this to become stronger?"

This isn't just about positive thinking. It's about understanding that your thoughts directly impact your actions. If you believe you have the power to create a good life, you'll take the steps necessary to make it happen. You'll push yourself out of your comfort zone, take risks, and keep moving forward even when things get tough.

The Power of Choice

Every day, you make countless choices. Some are small—what to eat, what to wear, how to spend your time. Others are bigger—what career path to follow, who to build relationships with, how to handle adversity. My father taught me that the quality of your life is determined by the choices you make, especially in the face of challenges.

When life throws obstacles in your way, you have a choice: you can either let them hold you back or use them as stepping stones to something greater. The choice is yours. It always has been. The key is to stop waiting for life to hand you success or happiness on a silver platter and start taking ownership of your future.

Do you want a better life? Then choose to take action. Choose to work hard. Choose to stay positive, even when it's hard. Choose to keep going, even when you want to quit. The power to create a fulfilling life isn't in some far-off dream—it's in your hands, right now.

Life Is What You Make It

There are no guarantees in life. You can't control what happens to you, but you can always control how you respond. You can either see life as something that happens to you or something that you create.

If you want a life filled with joy, purpose, and meaning, you have to be willing to put in the effort. That means taking responsibility for your happiness, growth, and success. It means choosing to see the good, even when life feels hard. It means deciding that, no matter what, you're going to live a life you're proud of.

"The Strength to Help Others and Celebrate Their Successes"

Lifting Others and Growing Together

The teachings of my father—principles of personal responsibility, gratitude, faith, and hard work—are not just about personal success. They are about creating a ripple effect, a way of living that not only elevates you but also uplifts those around you. As you've read in the previous chapters, life is as good as you want it to be, and that begins with how you approach your own life. But the greatest fulfillment comes when you use the strength you've gained to help others, celebrating their successes alongside your own.

This chapter is about the positive effects of embracing this lifestyle—how mastering self-discipline, gratitude, faith, and hard work can transform not just your own life, but your relationships, community, and ultimately, the world around you.

Better Relationships with Friends and Family

When you take responsibility for your life and embrace gratitude, hard work, and a positive mindset, something incredible happens: your relationships improve. My father often said, "Strength doesn't come from standing alone; it comes from knowing when to lift others up." This is the essence of true relationships—whether with friends, family, or coworkers. When you are strong, you have the capacity to strengthen others. When you live with gratitude, you appreciate those around you in ways that deepen your connections.

Gratitude alone can transform relationships. When you actively practice thankfulness, it shifts your focus from what others do wrong to what they do right. Rather than being quick to criticize or judge, you begin to appreciate the small acts of kindness, support, and love that those around you offer. This attitude fosters trust, communication, and a deep sense of mutual respect.

When you stop expecting others to be perfect and start recognizing the beauty in their efforts, your relationships blossom. You become a better listener, a more compassionate friend, and a more understanding partner. The strength you've gained from taking control of your own life gives you the patience and resilience to navigate difficult conversations or conflicts with grace. You no longer look to others for validation or fulfillment because you've built those things within yourself.

But it doesn't stop there. Lifting others becomes a natural extension of your own growth. When you take the time to help someone else—whether through encouragement, advice, or simply being there for them—you strengthen not only your relationship but also yourself. My father believed that helping others succeed was one of the greatest sources of fulfillment. Celebrating others doesn't diminish your own achievements—it amplifies them.

Discipline in Completing Personal Goals

Throughout this book, we've discussed the importance of discipline. Whether it's working hard early to enjoy life later or taking ownership of your mindset and actions, discipline is a cornerstone of a successful life. Here's the real secret: once you've mastered discipline in one area of your life, it spreads to every other area.

Let's say you've committed to working hard in your career, building a strong foundation for future success. The discipline you've developed—whether it's showing up on time, pushing through challenges, or staying focused—will naturally extend into your personal goals. Maybe you've always wanted to get fit, learn a new skill, or start a passion project. The self-discipline you've honed in one area will make it easier to achieve personal goals as well.

This kind of discipline is transformative because it creates momentum. The more you achieve, the more confident you become in your ability to set and reach new goals. Each success, no matter how small, reinforces the belief that you are capable of more. And here's the beautiful part: as you achieve your own goals, you inspire others to do the same. Your discipline becomes a model for those around you, showing them what's possible when you commit to your growth.

Trusting and Following God's Plan

One core message of this book is to "always be thankful for a good and loving God." This isn't just about practicing gratitude; it's about recognizing that a higher power guides you toward your purpose. When you trust in God's plan, you find peace even in the most challenging situations.

But trusting God's plan doesn't mean being passive. It means aligning your actions with your faith, knowing every step is part of a larger journey. When you follow the path laid out for you—one of gratitude, discipline, and hard work—you begin to see how God's hand is in everything. Even setbacks and challenges refine you, making you stronger and more resilient.

Faith gives you the courage to keep moving forward, even when the way isn't clear. It allows you to release control over the things you can't change and focus on what you can. When you live with faith, you trust that God is leading you exactly where you need to be. This trust allows you to take risks, step out of your comfort zone, and pursue your goals with confidence.

Living in alignment with God's plan inspires others to do the same. Your faith becomes a beacon for those who may be struggling to find their own path. By living with trust and gratitude, you show others the peace that comes from believing in something greater than themselves.

You may never know how deeply your faith impacts others, but your example can guide them toward spiritual growth.

Creating a Life of Meaning and Purpose

When you combine gratitude, discipline, faith, and a willingness to lift others up, you create a life of profound meaning and purpose. You become more than just a person living day to day—you become a source of light and strength for everyone around you. This lifestyle's ripple effect can change families, communities, and even the world.

As you continue to grow and achieve success, you naturally become someone who celebrates the successes of others. Rather than viewing life as a competition, you see it as a shared journey. You understand that when one person rises, we all rise. This mindset of abundance leads to a more fulfilling life, full of deep connections, meaningful achievements, and lasting impact.

My father's legacy wasn't just about the sayings he left behind—it was about the way he lived those sayings. He didn't just tell people to work hard or be grateful; he showed them what it looked like. His life was a testament to the power of lifting others up, staying disciplined in his goals, and helping others reach theirs.

As you move forward in your life, remember that your journey isn't just about you. It's about the people you inspire, the lives you touch, and the legacy you leave behind. When you live with gratitude, discipline, faith, and a commitment to helping others, you create a ripple effect that can change the world.

In the end, that's what life is about—lifting each other up, celebrating each other's victories, and walking the path together. When you do that, you not only fulfill your own potential, but you help others realize theirs as well. And that, my friend, is the greatest success of all.

"You Gotta Want Something" – The Power of Setting Goals in Life

My dad used to say, "You gotta want something, son." It was a phrase I heard countless times growing up, and it stuck with me. What he meant was simple but profound: if you don't have goals or something to strive for, you'll find yourself lost in a sea of idleness, drifting without direction. Wanting something—whether it's a dream, a passion, or simply a desire to be better—gives us the motivation to take action, move forward, and build the life we want.

My dad believed that goals weren't just important; they were essential. He taught me that having goals, no matter how big or small, keeps your mind sharp and your spirit focused. Goals give you a reason to wake up in the morning and take action. They push you to think about the future, to plan, and to make the most of your time. Without them, life can become aimless, filled with idle moments that, over time, can lead you down paths you never intended to walk.

Why Goals Matter: Keeping the Mind and Spirit Engaged

The essence of "You gotta want something" is that having a goal or a vision keeps your mind engaged and your spirit alive. Without goals, we fall into routines that can become stagnant, simply going through the motions of life without purpose or passion. Having a goal gives life meaning and direction.

Idle time, my dad used to say, is dangerous. It opens the door to distractions and temptations. When you're not actively working toward something, you're more likely to waste time through unhealthy habits, distractions, or slipping into negative thought patterns. Goals protect you from falling into that trap. They give you something to focus on, to work toward, and to achieve.

When we set goals, we keep our minds on positive, constructive matters. We take control of our time and use it to build something meaningful—whether that's a stronger body, a healthier relationship with God, a more fulfilling career, or a sense of peace and purpose. It doesn't matter what the goal is; what matters is that you want something, because that desire is what drives you forward.

Spiritual, Physical, and Mental Goals: Holistic Growth

My dad wasn't just talking about professional or material success when he said this. He believed in setting goals in all areas of life: spiritually, physically, and mentally. To live a full and meaningful life, you have to take care of all aspects of your being.

Spiritual Goals

Spiritual goals are about growth, connection, and alignment with something greater than ourselves. My dad often said that you can't live a fulfilled life if you aren't feeding your spirit. Whether it's deepening your faith, cultivating gratitude, or living in alignment with your values, spiritual goals keep you grounded and focused on what truly matters. They remind you that life isn't just about the material world—it's about something more profound, something that transcends the day-to-day struggles.

Setting spiritual goals might involve spending more time in prayer or meditation, seeking a deeper connection with God, or finding ways to serve and uplift others. These goals nourish your soul and provide a sense of peace and purpose that no external achievement can replace.

Physical Goals

My dad was also a big believer in taking care of the body. "Your body is the vessel that carries you through life, and if you don't take care of it, it won't take care of you." He often told me this as a reminder that physical health is a foundation for everything else we do. If you want to be mentally sharp, spiritually connected, and emotionally strong, you need to be physically well.

Setting physical goals could mean anything from exercising regularly to eating healthier or even sleeping better. It doesn't have to be about achieving a specific fitness milestone, but rather about creating habits that keep your body strong and healthy. A healthy body supports a healthy mind and spirit, and when all three are in harmony, you're able to live life to its fullest.

Mental Goals

Lastly, mental goals are about expanding your mind, cultivating resilience, and developing a positive outlook. My dad was a firm believer in continuous learning and growth. "You gotta want to be better, smarter, stronger—because life isn't going to wait for you to catch up," he'd say. Mental goals help you build the tools you need to face life's challenges with clarity and strength.

Setting mental goals might involve learning a new skill, reading more books, or working on mental resilience through mindfulness and stress management. It's about challenging your brain to grow, adapt, and become sharper every day. When your mind is engaged and growing, it's harder for negativity and doubt to take root.

Idle Time vs. Purposeful Action

Idle time is often the enemy of progress. When you don't have something you're working toward, it's easy to drift. My dad knew that when you're not focused on your goals, your mind wanders—and often, it doesn't wander to good places. Idle time is when we get stuck in negative patterns, whether through overthinking, indulging in unhealthy habits, or simply wasting time.

By having goals, you fill your time with purposeful action. You're not just passing time; you're building toward something meaningful. When you want something, your time is spent working toward it, and the more time you spend actively pursuing your goals, the less time you have for distractions, negativity, or self-doubt.

Goals give structure to your life. They create a roadmap, showing you where you're headed and why you're putting in the effort every day. Without that structure, it's easy to feel lost, unmotivated, or overwhelmed by the enormity of life's challenges. But with goals, every step you take is toward something greater—toward becoming the best version of yourself.

Going After Your Wants: Taking Action

It's not enough to want something; you have to go after it. My dad didn't just want me to dream—he wanted me to take action. He believed that a goal without action was just a wish, and wishes wouldn't get you anywhere.

This is the heart of his lesson: desire must be paired with action. If you want something, you have to be willing to put in the work. Whether it's getting up early to train for a marathon, spending extra time studying for an exam, or praying every morning to deepen your spiritual connection, action is what turns your desires into reality.

My dad taught me that it wasn't just about achieving the goal itself. The journey toward that goal was just as important, if not more so. The lessons learned along the way—discipline, patience, resilience— were what truly mattered. Going after your wants wasn't about instant gratification; it was about building a life that aligned with your values, your desires, and your purpose.

The Impact of Goals on Life: Fulfillment and Joy

When you live a life driven by goals, you experience a deeper sense of fulfillment and joy. You're not just surviving—you're thriving. Every day has meaning because you're working toward something greater, something that excites and motivates you.

The goals you set shape the person you become. They push you to grow, step outside your comfort zone, and challenge yourself. And as you achieve those goals—no matter how small—you build confidence and a sense of accomplishment that fuels your desire to keep going.

"You gotta want something" wasn't just my dad's way of telling me to dream big—it was his way of reminding me that life is about progress, about moving forward, and about becoming the person you're meant to be. When you live a life full of goals—whether spiritual, physical, or mental—you fill your life with meaning, purpose, and joy.

Live with Purpose, Go After What You Want

In every aspect of life, "You gotta want something" should be your mantra. Set goals in every area of your life: spiritual, physical, and mental. Want to be better. Want to grow. Want to make a difference. And then take the steps to go after those desires. Because it's not enough to want something—you have to take action, build discipline, and commit to the process.

Your goals are what keep you moving forward, and they are the key to living a life full of purpose, fulfillment, and joy.

"Wanting Isn't Enough—Do the Things It Takes"

It wasn't just about wanting something. My dad made that clear from the beginning. He would always say, "You gotta want something, son, but wanting isn't enough—you gotta DO the things it takes to get what you want."

It's a powerful truth that goes beyond simple desire. My dad believed that while having goals was essential, they were meaningless without action. Wanting something—whether it's a better life, success, sobriety, or healing—doesn't accomplish anything on its own. It's the action we take in pursuit of those goals that creates change. My dad wanted everyone he helped to understand this: Your dreams don't come true by wishing for them; they come true by working for them.

The Difference Between Wanting and Doing

One of the things my dad saw repeatedly in his work with people struggling through addiction, pain, and life's hardships was that many of them wanted change, but they weren't willing to do what it took to make that change happen. They wanted to be free from addiction, they wanted peace in their lives, they wanted to get out of the situations they were in—but "wanting" alone never got them there. My dad understood that the desire to change is only the first step in a long journey.

Desire without action is just a wish.

It's easy to fall into the trap of wanting things to be better but never taking the steps necessary to make it happen. Wanting something feels good—it's hopeful, it's inspiring—but it's also passive. My dad knew that lasting change required more than just hope; it required hard work, discipline, and a commitment to take action even when it's uncomfortable.

He would often tell me, "Son, you can want something all day long, but if you don't get up and do the work, it's never going to happen. You have to be willing to put in the effort, to push through the hard times, and to make it happen for yourself."

This is where many people fall short. They have dreams, but they're afraid of the sacrifices it takes to achieve those dreams. They want the result, but they don't want the struggle. They want success, but they don't want the grind. My dad's message was clear: if you want something, you have to DO the work to get it.

"Thou Shalt Not Want"—A Biblical Perspective on Action

My dad's approach also tied into his deep faith. He often referenced the Bible when working with people who were struggling, reminding them of the wisdom found in scripture. One verse he connected to this message was from Psalm 23:1: "The Lord is my shepherd; I shall not want." This verse speaks to the idea that God provides everything we need. In my dad's eyes, this wasn't just about material provision—it was about the fact that God gave us the tools, the resources, and the abilities to create the life we want. We don't have to live in want because God has already equipped us with everything we need to act.

For my dad, this verse wasn't about sitting back and waiting for things to happen. It was about recognizing that God has already given us what we need to take action. We are empowered by God to do, to work, to create, and to change.

"God gave you the ability to do whatever you want, to get whatever you need, so there is nothing to want when you can do something about it."

This was my dad's belief. He didn't want people to live in a state of longing or dissatisfaction because they weren't taking responsibility for the gifts and abilities God had given them. He would tell the people he worked with that they were capable of great things, but it required them to step up, take control, and DO the work.

Action Creates Change: Doing What It Takes

For my dad, taking action wasn't just about working hard in a job or pursuing success in the traditional sense. It was about doing whatever it took in every area of life—spiritually, physically, mentally, and emotionally. He encouraged people to set goals, but more importantly, he pushed them to take steps every day to move toward those goals.

In the lives of the people he helped, this often meant starting with small, achievable actions that built momentum over time. For someone in recovery, it might mean attending meetings consistently, getting up early to pray, or calling a friend instead of reaching for a drink. For someone trying to change their life, it could mean looking for job opportunities, learning new skills, or setting healthy boundaries with people who pulled them down.

My dad believed that every small action added up to big change over time. It didn't matter if the steps were tiny, as long as you kept moving forward. Every time you chose to DO something rather than stay idle, you were investing in your future.

And he knew that for many of the people he worked with, those small steps were hard. Recovery, healing, rebuilding a life—these weren't easy journeys. But he also knew that it was those difficult steps that made the difference between those who wanted change and those who actually achieved it.

Breaking Free from Idle Time

One of the key things my dad fought against was idle time. He believed that when people weren't actively working toward something, their lives tended to drift into dangerous territory. Idle time led to negative thoughts, bad decisions, and a lack of purpose.

For those struggling with addiction, idleness was a trap that could easily lead to relapse. For people feeling lost or uncertain, idle time often resulted in spiraling into despair or hopelessness. "You gotta keep moving, son. You gotta keep doing. Idle hands will lead you down a path you don't want to go."

This belief drove him to keep people engaged, to encourage them to fill their time with positive actions. Whether it was going for a walk, reading a book, connecting with a support group, or finding a job—doing something was always better than doing nothing.

Taking Ownership of Your Wants

Ultimately, my dad's message wasn't just about wanting or doing—it was about taking ownership of your life. He wanted people to understand that their lives weren't something that just happened to them. They had power. They had control. And if they weren't happy with where they were, they had the ability to change it by taking action.

"If you want something, take responsibility for getting it. Don't wait for someone else to hand it to you. Don't expect it to fall into your lap. Get up and go after it."

This was my dad's philosophy, and it's a lesson that I've carried with me throughout my life. It's something he instilled in everyone he helped. He didn't believe in excuses. He believed in action. He believed in the power of taking control of your life, your circumstances, and your future.

From Wanting to Doing

Wanting something is the first step—but it's only the beginning. True change happens when you pair your desire with action. When you take control of your life, make a plan, and take steps every day to get closer to what you want, you turn your wants into reality.

"Thou shalt not want," my dad would remind us, not because we should give up on our desires, but because God has already given us everything we need to achieve them. We are empowered to act, to do, to make things happen. And when we live this way—when we stop wanting and start doing—we unlock the potential for a life filled with purpose, fulfillment, and joy.

"Save Something from Every Paycheck" – The Discipline of Small, Consistent Actions

My dad used to say, "Save something from every paycheck." On the surface, it was about building financial security—putting aside money for the future, even if it was just a few dollars. But, like most of my dad's sayings, there was a deeper meaning beneath the surface. This wasn't just about saving money; it was about cultivating discipline in every area of life.

"If we can faithfully pay our bills every month, we can faithfully pay ourselves too," he would remind me. Whether it was $5 or $500, the act of saving was a discipline that went beyond just dollars and cents. It was about taking care of your future self and building a habit of consistency that would serve you in all aspects of life.

The Power of Discipline: Building Habits That Last

For my dad, discipline was the foundation of success. It wasn't about reaching goals immediately or achieving everything at once; it was about showing up consistently, putting in the effort day after day, and trusting that the results would come over time. Saving something from every paycheck was a small, tangible way to practice that discipline, but the lessons it taught went far beyond finances.

The act of setting aside money, even if it was just a few dollars, required self-control. It meant prioritizing long-term security over short-term gratification. It meant resisting the urge to spend impulsively and instead thinking about the future. More importantly, it built a habit of discipline that spilled over into other areas of life.

My dad used to say, "Self-discipline is the key to happiness." At first, that might sound counterintuitive—after all, discipline sounds like hard work, sacrifice, and sometimes doing things you don't want to do. But he was right. Discipline creates structure, and within that structure, we find freedom and happiness. When you develop the discipline to save money, to take care of your health, or to pursue your goals, you create a life that is stable, secure, and fulfilling.

Discipline Leads to Accomplishment

One of the key things my dad believed was that discipline leads to accomplishment, even when you don't meet your goals. That's because the real success isn't always in the outcome—it's in the attempt. It's in the process of showing up, doing the work, and giving it your all.

He would tell me, "The success was always in the attempt. You will never make the shot that you don't shoot."

This meant that even if you didn't hit the target, the act of trying, of putting in the effort, was its own form of success. When you practice discipline, you build confidence in yourself. You know that you gave it your best, and that knowledge gives you a sense of accomplishment, even if things didn't turn out the way you hoped.

This lesson applied to so much more than just saving money. It applied to every area of life—whether it was pursuing a new career, sticking with a fitness routine, or working on personal growth. Discipline builds resilience, and resilience is what carries you through the inevitable setbacks and failures that come with life.

For the people my dad helped, this was a crucial lesson. Many of them had faced hardship, addiction, or financial struggles, and they felt like they had failed time and time again. My dad would remind them that the attempt itself was a victory. Just by showing up, just by trying to get better, they were already succeeding. It wasn't about perfection; it was about progress, about doing the best you could with what you had, one step at a time.

The Ripple Effect of Small Actions

Another key element of my dad's lesson was that small, consistent actions add up over time. Saving something from every paycheck wasn't just about building financial security; it was about building habits that led to long-term success.

"You might think $5 isn't much," he'd say, "but it's the discipline behind it that counts. If you can do it with $5, you can do it with $500."

It was never about the amount of money; it was about the act of saving, the act of committing to a goal, and sticking with it. That small action, repeated consistently, created a ripple effect that led to bigger changes over time. The same principle applied to other areas of life: if you could discipline yourself to go for a 10-minute walk every day, eventually that walk might turn into a workout routine that transforms your health. If you could discipline yourself to read 10 pages of a book each day, over time, you'd finish dozens of books, and your knowledge and perspective would grow exponentially.

Small actions, done consistently, lead to big results.

The key was to focus on the process, not just the outcome. My dad knew that if you trusted the process—if you stayed disciplined and kept showing up—the results would come, even if they weren't immediate.

Saving as an Act of Faith

There was also a spiritual element to my dad's teaching on saving. Saving was an act of faith—faith in the future, faith in yourself, and faith in the idea that small actions would lead to something greater.

My dad believed that saving money, no matter how small the amount, was a way of saying, "I believe in tomorrow. I believe in the future, and I'm taking steps to prepare for it." It was a way of putting your faith into action, of trusting that the seeds you planted today would grow into something worthwhile down the road.

This kind of faith wasn't just about finances; it was about life. Whether you were investing in your health, your relationships, or your spiritual growth, the act of saving—of putting something aside, of making an investment in the future—was a way of acknowledging that you had the power to shape your own destiny.

For the people he helped, my dad often emphasized this idea. He knew that many of them had lost hope, that they felt like their future was out of their control. But by teaching them to save, even if it was just a small amount, he was showing them that they still had power. They still had the ability to take action, to create a better future for themselves.

Discipline and Happiness: The Keys to Consistent Growth

At the core of my dad's lesson was the belief that discipline and happiness are interconnected. He believed that when you practice discipline—whether through saving money, taking care of your body, or working toward your goals—you create a sense of accomplishment and fulfillment that brings lasting happiness.

Discipline isn't about being rigid or depriving yourself of joy. It's about having the self-control to make choices that align with your values and your long-term goals. When you live with discipline, you build a life that reflects who you truly are. You make decisions that lead to growth, that bring you closer to your potential, and that allow you to live with integrity.

Happiness isn't about always achieving your goals; it's about knowing that you gave it your all. When you live with discipline, you can look back on your efforts with pride, even if you didn't always hit the mark. You know that you put in the work, that you stayed consistent, and that you gave it everything you had. That sense of accomplishment, of doing your best, is what brings true happiness.

You Will Never Make the Shot You Don't Shoot

One of the most important lessons my dad taught me was that "You will never make the shot you don't shoot." This was his way of saying that you have to take action if you want to succeed. Sitting on the sidelines, waiting for things to happen, or being too afraid to try will never get you anywhere.

Whether it was about saving money, starting a new business, or pursuing a personal goal, my dad always encouraged people to take the shot. Even if you fail, even if you miss the target, the act of trying is what matters.

The people my dad worked with often felt paralyzed by fear—fear of failure, fear of rejection, fear of the unknown. But he would remind them that not trying was the only real failure. Success wasn't about always hitting the mark; it was about showing up, giving it your all, and having the courage to take the shot.

Save, Discipline, and Shoot Your Shot

The saying "Save something from every paycheck" was never just about money. It was about building discipline, creating habits, and taking action. It was about recognizing that small, consistent steps lead to big results, and that success isn't always about achieving your goals—it's about the discipline you build along the way.

In every aspect of life, from finances to personal growth to relationships, the key is to keep showing up, to keep taking action, and to trust that the process will lead you where you need to go.

"You will never make the shot you don't shoot," my dad would say, reminding us all that the real success lies in the attempt. So save, build discipline, and shoot your shot.

"You Always Have the Power to Change Your Mind" – The Courage to Embrace New Paths

My dad had a saying that resonated deeply with me throughout my life: "You always have the power to change your mind." At first, this might sound like advice to avoid commitment or second-guess your decisions, but it was actually about something far more important. It was about staying open to new information, learning from experience, and having the courage to change course when necessary.

What my dad meant was that we're never truly locked into any path—especially not the ones we've chosen for ourselves. Life is full of twists and turns, and sometimes, the decisions we made with good intentions or careful thought lead us to places we didn't expect. My dad taught me that the power to change your mind wasn't a sign of weakness—it was a sign of wisdom and strength.

"Thoroughly think through things before making your decisions to avoid waffling back and forth, but if you see a better way to achieve what you're trying to do, always stay open-minded to positive change if it makes sense."

This was my dad's way of saying that while commitment and follow-through are important, so is flexibility. We must learn to balance careful decision-making with the willingness to adapt when circumstances change or when we realize there's a better way forward.

The Trap of Stubbornness: When Pride Hurts You

One of the most dangerous things my dad warned against was pride. Pride can often keep us stuck in places we don't want to be. It can make us cling to decisions that no longer serve us simply because we don't want to admit we were wrong or because we fear what others might think.

"Pride will always hurt you," he would say, and he was right. Pride makes us dig in our heels when we should be moving forward. It makes us hold on to outdated beliefs, habits, or decisions, even when, deep down, we know they're not working. Pride tells us that changing our mind is a sign of failure when, in reality, changing our mind can be the smartest thing we can do.

In his work with people in recovery or those facing life's hardships, my dad saw this all the time. People would make decisions—sometimes bad ones—and they would stick with those decisions far longer than they should, simply because they didn't want to admit they had made a mistake. They were afraid of looking weak or indecisive, so they doubled down on choices that were hurting them.

But my dad would remind them, "You have the power to change your mind. It's never too late to do something different."

This was a powerful message, especially for people who felt trapped by their past decisions. It gave them permission to let go of choices that weren't serving them, to pivot, and to try a new path. It wasn't about being indecisive or flaky—it was about having the courage to recognize when change was necessary and embracing it with humility.

The Balance Between Commitment and Flexibility

One of the most important lessons my dad taught me was the balance between commitment and flexibility. He wasn't saying you should constantly change your mind or waffle back and forth between decisions. He believed in the value of careful, thoughtful decision-making. He wanted me to think things through, weigh my options, and commit to my choices with intention.

But at the same time, he wanted me to understand that life is unpredictable. Sometimes, even the best-laid plans don't work out the way we expect. Sometimes, new information comes to light, or our circumstances change in ways we couldn't have anticipated. In those moments, the ability to change your mind is a strength, not a weakness.

"You don't have to be stubborn in your decisions," he would say. "You just have to be smart."

For my dad, being smart meant being willing to adapt when necessary. It meant understanding that life isn't always black and white—there's often a middle ground between sticking to your commitments and knowing when to pivot. The key was to stay open-minded, to stay humble, and to always be willing to consider a better way if it made sense.

Open-Mindedness as a Tool for Growth

My dad's saying also taught me about the importance of open-mindedness. He believed that if you approached life with a rigid mindset—never willing to change or evolve—you would end up missing out on growth opportunities. Being open to new ideas, new ways of thinking, and new ways of doing things was essential for personal development.

"If you think you've got everything figured out, you'll never learn anything new," he would say. "You always have the power to change your mind, and that's how you grow."

For my dad, being open-minded didn't mean being wishy-washy or unsure of yourself. It meant being willing to learn from experience, from other people, and from the lessons life throws at you. It meant being humble enough to admit that you don't have all the answers and that sometimes, the best thing you can do is take a step back, reconsider, and change course.

How Changing Your Mind Can Lead to Positive Change

One of the most powerful aspects of this lesson was how it encouraged positive change. So many people, especially those struggling with addiction or difficult circumstances, felt like they were stuck. They had made decisions in the past that led them down dark paths, and they didn't see a way out. But my dad's saying, "You always have the power to change your mind," was a reminder that they could choose a different path at any moment.

For the people my dad helped, this was a lifeline. It gave them hope that their lives didn't have to be defined by their past choices. It reminded them that no matter how far down the wrong road you've gone, you can always turn around.

This applied to all areas of life—whether it was relationships, careers, health, or personal growth. The message was simple: you're never trapped. If the path you're on isn't leading you where you want to go, you can change direction. You can make a new choice. And sometimes, that new choice leads to something better than you could have ever imagined.

Letting Go of Pride

One of the hardest things for people to do is let go of pride. Pride tells us that we have to stick with our decisions, even when they're hurting us. Pride makes us feel like changing our mind is a sign of weakness or failure. But my dad knew that pride was often the biggest obstacle to growth.

"Pride will always hurt you," he would say, "because it keeps you stuck in places you don't need to be."

Letting go of pride requires humility. It requires admitting that you don't have all the answers and that sometimes, the best thing you can do is admit that you need to change direction. But my dad believed that there was strength in that kind of humility. Changing your mind wasn't about giving up—it was about choosing the path that leads to the best outcome.

For the people my dad helped, this often meant letting go of their pride and accepting help, even when it felt uncomfortable. It meant admitting that their way wasn't working and being open to new methods, new ideas, or new support systems. And in doing so, they found new ways to grow, heal, and move forward.

Think Before You Choose, But Be Willing to Pivot

My dad's message was about balance. He wanted people to think carefully before making decisions—to weigh the pros and cons, to consider their options, and to commit to their choices with intention. But he also wanted them to understand that being willing to pivot when necessary was a sign of wisdom.

"You don't have to be locked into your decisions," he'd say. "If there's a better way, be open to it."

This philosophy helped countless people my dad worked with. It reminded them that they didn't have to stick with choices that weren't serving them and that life is about growth, learning, and adapting. Changing your mind, when done for the right reasons, can open doors to new opportunities, new ways of thinking, and new paths to success.

The Power of Humility and Growth

In life, you will face many decisions. Some will lead you to great success, and others may not turn out the way you hoped. But my dad's lesson, "You always have the power to change your mind," is a reminder that no decision is final. You have the ability to learn, to grow, and to pivot when necessary.

Let go of pride. Stay open to new possibilities. And remember that true wisdom lies in the balance between thoughtful decision-making and the flexibility to embrace change.

When you live with this mindset, you allow yourself the freedom to grow, to evolve, and to make choices that lead to a life filled with purpose and fulfillment.

"You Are What You Are Around" – The Power of Your Circle

One of my dad's most impactful sayings was, "You are what you are around. Hang with trash, you're gonna stink."

It was a blunt, no-nonsense way of saying that the people, environments, and influences you surround yourself with shape who you are, whether you like it or not. The people you spend time with, the thoughts you entertain, and the behaviors you allow into your life—all of these rub off on you. Even if you think you're immune to their influence, over time, these things start to shape your mindset, your habits, and your future.

My dad believed that if you want to be the best version of yourself, you have to stay around people, ideas, and environments that contribute to your growth—people who lift you up, challenge you to be better, and encourage your progress. Just as importantly, you need to remove yourself from influences that bring you down, drain your energy, or hold you back.

The Influence of Your Circle

My dad saw firsthand how the people in someone's life could either elevate them or drag them down. In his work with those recovering from addiction, he noticed a common pattern: many people fell into destructive habits not because they were inherently bad or weak, but because of the people they were surrounded by. The wrong crowd—those who encouraged bad habits, destructive behaviors, and negative mindsets—often played a major role in their downfall.

But the opposite was also true. When people surrounded themselves with supportive, positive, and goal-oriented individuals, they were more likely to succeed in their recovery and in life. The people in your circle have a direct impact on your mindset, your habits, and your progress. It's impossible to be around negativity all the time without being affected by it.

My dad would often say, "You can't hang around trash and expect to come out smelling like roses. If you surround yourself with negativity, laziness, or toxic people, that's going to rub off on you eventually."

He wasn't just talking about extreme cases—he meant this in every aspect of life. Even small influences, the little things people say or do, can seep into your own thinking and behavior. If you're surrounded by people who constantly complain, gossip, or make excuses, you'll start to adopt those same mindsets, even if you don't realize it at first.

Your Circle Shapes Your Thinking

It's not just the people in your life that matter—it's also the ideas, thoughts, and mentalities you surround yourself with. If you're constantly exposed to negativity, pessimism, or limiting beliefs, those ideas will start to shape your worldview. You'll begin to believe that success is out of reach, that change is impossible, or that you're not capable of achieving your goals.

"You are what you think," my dad would remind me, "and what you think is influenced by what's around you."

This was his way of saying that your thoughts are shaped by the people you talk to, the media you consume, the conversations you engage in, and the environments you live in. If you want to elevate your thinking, you have to be intentional about surrounding yourself with positive influences—people who think big, who have a growth mindset, and who push you to believe in your potential.

Your circle should be pulling you up to another level, not dragging you down. That's why it's so important to be selective about who and what you allow into your life. If the people around you aren't helping you grow, they're probably holding you back.

The Power of Positive Influence

One of the most profound lessons my dad taught me was that positive influence creates positive change. When you surround yourself with people who are ambitious, driven, and supportive, you naturally start to adopt those qualities yourself. Their success, mindset, and energy become contagious.

My dad saw this happen all the time with the people he helped. When someone in recovery surrounded themselves with others who were also working to improve their lives—people who were committed to their sobriety, personal growth, and healing—they were far more likely to succeed. The collective energy of positive influence created a momentum that pushed everyone forward.

But it wasn't just about avoiding negative people. My dad believed that if you wanted to grow, you had to seek out people who were better than you in some way—people who were further along in their journey, more knowledgeable, or more disciplined. These people would challenge you to rise to their level, push beyond your current limitations, and keep growing.

He would say, "You need to be around people who make you uncomfortable in a good way—people who make you think bigger, work harder, and become better." These were the kinds of people who would pull you up, not just support you where you were.

The Dangers of Staying Around Negativity

On the flip side, my dad knew the dangers of staying around negative or toxic people. "Hang with trash, you're gonna stink," he'd say, and it was true. No matter how strong your intentions or how disciplined you are, if you surround yourself with people who drag you down, you'll eventually start to sink to their level.

Negativity is like a virus. It spreads quickly and infects everything around it. If you're constantly exposed to people who are bitter, pessimistic, or toxic, you'll find yourself adopting those same attitudes. Even if you're aware of their influence, it's hard to stay positive and focused when negativity is always in your ear.

For many of the people my dad helped, this was one of the hardest lessons to learn. They had to let go of toxic relationships, even if it meant losing old friends or distancing themselves from family members who weren't supportive of their growth. It wasn't easy, but it was necessary. My dad would remind them that you can't move forward if you're surrounded by people who are pulling you backward.

Letting go of negative influences is an act of self-respect. It's about recognizing your worth and surrounding yourself with people who see and support that worth. If your circle isn't helping you grow, it's time to find a new circle.

Choosing Your Circle Wisely

One of the most important decisions you'll make in life is who you choose to surround yourself with. My dad was very intentional about the people he allowed into his life, and he encouraged me to do the same. He taught me to choose friends and mentors who were aligned with my values, goals, and vision for the future.

He wasn't saying you had to cut out everyone who wasn't perfect or walk away from relationships as soon as they hit a rough patch. But he was saying that you need to be mindful of the overall influence people have on your life. If they consistently bring negativity, toxicity, or drama, it's time to reconsider their role in your journey.

My dad also believed in the importance of surrounding yourself with people who challenge you to grow. Your circle shouldn't just be a group of people who make you feel comfortable or who always agree with you. It should include people who push you to think bigger, work harder, and become the best version of yourself.

He often said, "Your friends should be pulling you up, not holding you down." This meant seeking out relationships with people striving for greatness in their own lives and who would encourage you to do the same. It meant finding mentors who had already achieved the things you wanted to achieve and learning from their experiences.

Mind Your Thoughts, Too

In addition to choosing your circle wisely, my dad also taught me the importance of being mindful of my thoughts. He believed that just like the people you surround yourself with, the thoughts you entertain can either elevate you or bring you down.

"You are what you think," he'd say, and it was true. The thoughts you allow to take root in your mind shape your beliefs, your actions, and your reality. If you're constantly feeding your mind with negativity, doubt, or fear, those thoughts will start to manifest in your life.

My dad encouraged me to surround myself with positive thoughts, uplifting ideas, and empowering beliefs. This meant being intentional about the books I read, the conversations I had, and the content I consumed. It wasn't just about avoiding negative people—it was about creating an environment of positivity in every aspect of my life.

You Are the Company You Keep

In life, the people, environments, and thoughts you surround yourself with have a profound influence on who you become. My dad's saying, "You are what you are around. Hang with trash, you're gonna stink," is a reminder of the power of those influences—whether we recognize them or not. Just as the company you keep can lift you up, it can also pull you down.

To live a life of growth and purpose, you must be intentional about your circle. Choose to surround yourself with people who challenge you, encourage you, and push you to be better. Fill your mind with ideas that expand your vision, uplift your spirit, and help you strive for more. Whether it's friends, mentors, colleagues, or the thoughts you dwell on daily, the quality of your environment will shape your path.

But this isn't just about avoiding negative people—it's about seeking out relationships and influences that pull you up to new heights. Your circle should inspire you to grow, reach for more, and live in alignment with your goals.

Remember, just as you are shaped by those around you, you also have the power to shape your own environment. Be mindful of who and what you let into your life. Surround yourself with positivity, ambition, and people who reflect the best version of who you are and who you want to become.

Ultimately, you are the company you keep—so choose your circle wisely, because it will define the person you grow into.

www.ingramcontent.com/pod-product-compliance
Lightning Source LLC
Chambersburg PA
CBHW061703120626
46550CB00003B/1063